CAMBRIDGE LIBRARY COLLECTION

Books of enduring scholarly value

Archaeology

The discovery of material remains from the recent or the ancient past has always been a source of fascination, but the development of archaeology as an academic discipline which interpreted such finds is relatively recent. It was the work of Winckelmann at Pompeii in the 1760s which first revealed the potential of systematic excavation to scholars and the wider public. Pioneering figures of the nineteenth century such as Schliemann, Layard and Petrie transformed archaeology from a search for ancient artifacts, by means as crude as using gunpowder to break into a tomb, to a science which drew from a wide range of disciplines - ancient languages and literature, geology, chemistry, social history - to increase our understanding of human life and society in the remote past.

The Wallet-Book of the Roman Wall

After the success of his 1851 book on the Roman Wall (also reissued in this series), in 1863 John Collingwood Bruce (1805–92) published this shorter work, intended as 'a guide to pilgrims journeying along the Barrier of the Lower Isthmus'. Designed 'for the field, not the library table', it sought 'to inform the traveller what he is to look for, and to assist him in examining it'. Bruce first gives a short history of the wall, including medieval and more recent accounts, and then an overview of the 73-mile structure itself, from Wallsend in the east to Bowness in the west. The remainder of the book, illustrated with maps and line engravings, leads the traveller from section to section, noting details such as the re-use of Roman masonry in more recent buildings. This guide was enormously popular, and newly revised versions continue to be published in the twenty-first century.

Cambridge University Press has long been a pioneer in the reissuing of out-of-print titles from its own backlist, producing digital reprints of books that are still sought after by scholars and students but could not be reprinted economically using traditional technology. The Cambridge Library Collection extends this activity to a wider range of books which are still of importance to researchers and professionals, either for the source material they contain, or as landmarks in the history of their academic discipline.

Drawing from the world-renowned collections in the Cambridge University Library and other partner libraries, and guided by the advice of experts in each subject area, Cambridge University Press is using state-of-the-art scanning machines in its own Printing House to capture the content of each book selected for inclusion. The files are processed to give a consistently clear, crisp image, and the books finished to the high quality standard for which the Press is recognised around the world. The latest print-on-demand technology ensures that the books will remain available indefinitely, and that orders for single or multiple copies can quickly be supplied.

The Cambridge Library Collection brings back to life books of enduring scholarly value (including out-of-copyright works originally issued by other publishers) across a wide range of disciplines in the humanities and social sciences and in science and technology.

The Wallet-Book of the Roman Wall

A Guide to Pilgrims Journeying along the Barrier of the Lower Isthmus

John Collingwood Bruce

Cambridge University Press

CAMBRIDGE
UNIVERSITY PRESS

University Printing House, Cambridge, CB2 8BS, United Kingdom

Cambridge University Press is part of the University of Cambridge.
It furthers the University's mission by disseminating knowledge in the pursuit of education, learning and research at the highest international levels of excellence.

www.cambridge.org
Information on this title: www.cambridge.org/9781108080668

This edition first published 1863
This digitally printed version 2015

ISBN 978-1-108-08066-8 Paperback

The original edition of this book contains a number of colour plates, which have been reproduced in black and white. Colour versions of these images can be found online at www.cambridge.org/9781108080668

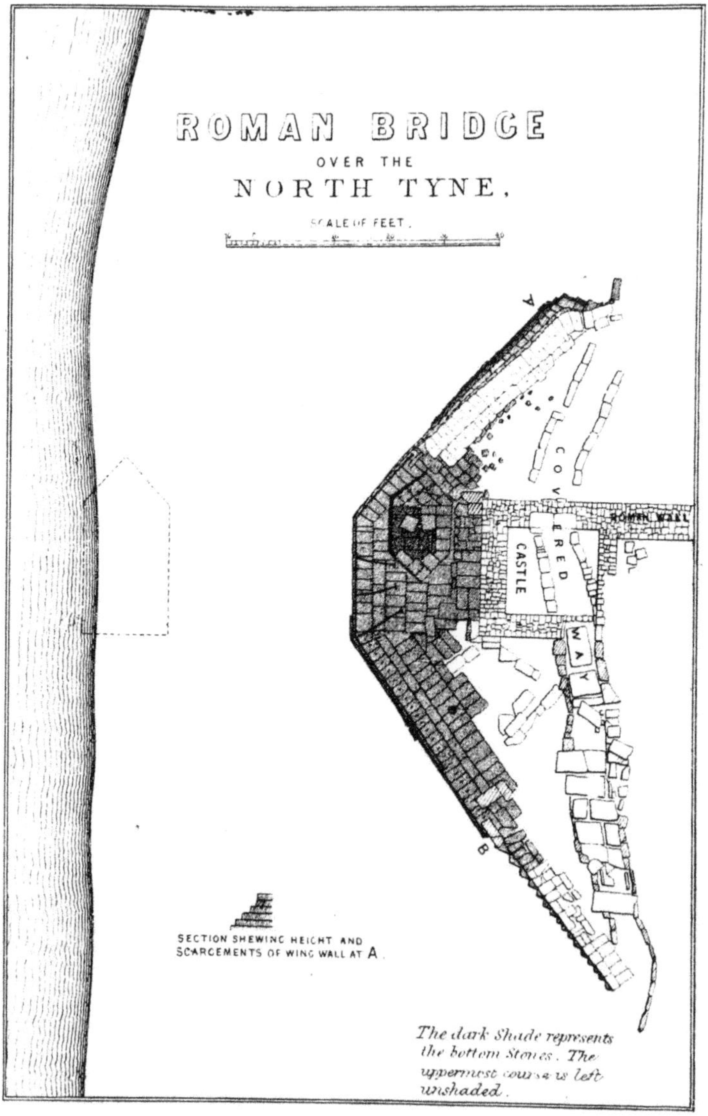
ROMAN BRIDGE
OVER THE
NORTH TYNE.
SCALE OF FEET.
A
B
COVERED WAY
CASTLE
ROMAN WALL
SECTION SHEWING HEIGHT AND SCARCEMENTS OF WING WALL AT A.
The dark Shade represents the bottom Stones. The uppermost course is left unshaded.

THE

WALLET-BOOK

OF

THE ROMAN WALL,

A GUIDE

TO

PILGRIMS JOURNEYING ALONG THE BARRIER OF THE LOWER ISTHMUS.

BY THE

REV. J. COLLINGWOOD BRUCE, LL.D., F.S.A.

LONDON :
LONGMAN, GREEN, LONGMAN, ROBERTS, & GREEN.

NEWCASTLE-UPON-TYNE :
D. H. WILSON, GREY STREET.

1863.

NEWCASTLE-UPON-TYNE:
PRINTED BY J. G. FORSTER, CLAYTON STREET.

PREFACE.

CAMDEN, speaking of the Roman works in Britain, says "Certes, they are works of exceeding great admiration, and sumptuous magnificence; especially the Picts' Wall." Stukeley in his *Iter Boreale* denominates the Wall "The noblest monument in Europe." Hutton of Birmingham made the tour of the Wall on foot in his 79th year; and has left us an account of his journey, which is full of youthful enthusiasm.

At one time Camden, Stukeley, and Hutton had but few followers—now, the general diffusion of knowledge, the interest felt by Englishmen in the history of their own country, and a better appreciation of the value of antiquarian research, have awakened a desire in many carefully to examine the Barrier of the Lower Isthmus from sea to sea. Once more the language of Chaucer is applicable:—

> "Then longen folk to go on pilgrimages."

To assist such, this little work has been prepared. It is intended for the field, not the library table.

It does not profess to describe the various objects visited, but to inform the traveller what he is to look for, and to assist him in examining it.

The writer may be allowed to refer those who wish for a fuller description of the Barrier and its antiquities, to his work upon "The Roman Wall," a third edition of which has been some years in preparation, and will ere long be issued.

He hopes soon also to put into the hands of antiquaries a treatise upon the "Inscribed and Sculptured Stones of the Roman Era" which have been found in the North of England; in the preparation of which he has derived most important assistance from some of the learned and the noble of the land.

Newcastle-upon-Tyne,
15 *July*, 1863.

TABLE OF CONTENTS.

LIST OF ILLUSTRATIONS.

Those marked * are lithographs; the rest are wood-engravings.

THE

Wallet-book of the Roman Wall.

CHAPTER I.

INTRODUCTORY.

He who contemplates a pilgrimage *per lineam Valli*, if he be imbued with a thorough love of antiquity, and duly appreciate the importance of the great structure which invites his attention, will not lightly enter upon his enterprise. Before attaching the scallop-shell to his hat and adjusting his wallet, he will probably wish to review the earliest chapter of our British history, and ascertain the state of things in this land before King Arthur ruled. Perchance, too, he may wish to carry with him upon his journey, in the form of *memoranda*, some of the results of his reading. To direct him in his earlier inquiries, and to supply him with some materials for subsequent reference, the following sections of this chapter are set before him. Equipment.

I.—Works upon the Subject.

Camden, in his *Britannia*, besides describing the inscriptions under the various localities where they were Camden's Britannia.

found, has a short chapter headed "*Vallum, sive Murus Picticus.*" The last edition printed in the author's life time is that of 1607. The *Britannia* was translated by Dr. Philemon Holland under, as is understood, the supervision of the author. The edition of 1637, contains the cuts and plates of the last Latin edition. Bishop Gibson published in 1695 a new translation of Camden's *Britannia*, with "additions and improvements." A fourth edition appeared in 1772. The Bishop's additions unhappily are not always improvements. The work contains a chapter on the Wall, written by a person who surveyed it in 1708. This writer is the earliest who having traversed the whole length of the structure, has given us an account of it. The editions of Camden most in vogue at present, are those by Richard Gough, the one published in 3 vols., fol., 1798; the other in 4 vols., fol., 1806.

Gordon. The *Itinerarium Septentrionale, or a Journey through most of the Counties of Scotland,* and those in the North of England, was published by Alexander Gordon, 1727. He is the Sandy Gordon of Scott's *Antiquary*. Gordon traversed portions of the Wall in company with Horsley.

Horsley's Britannia. Horsley's *Britannia Romana*, published in 1732, is still the great store-house of information on the Roman Antiquities of Britain. He has treated of the Wall and its inscriptions largely and lucidly. Unfortunately, his engravings, for the most part, do great injustice to the altars and sculptures which they represent.

Warburton. Warburton's *Vallum Romanum*, published in 1753, consists of those portions of Horsley's work which bear directly upon the Wall, transferred to his own book, with the smallest possible acknowledgement. It has the advantage over the *Britannia Romana* of being portable.

In 1776, some years after the death of its author, Stukeley's "*Iter Boreale*" was published. It contains the memoranda of a journey taken in 1725, in the company of Mr. Roger Gale, over the western and northern parts of England. His account of the Wall is interesting—many of his remarks being as original as they are just. **Stukeley.**

Brand, in an Appendix to the first volume of his *History of Newcastle*, published in 1789, gives a brief account of the Wall. **Brand.**

William Hutton, of Birmingham, in the year 1801, at the age of 78, traversed the great Barrier on foot, and gave to the world the result of his observations in a work entitled *The History of the Roman Wall.* Though the work betrays some of the characteristics of the advanced age of the writer, yet a fine vein of enthusiasm runs through it. **Hutton.**

The Rev. John Hodgson, who was at the time incumbent of Jarrow and Heworth, published, in *The Picture of Newcastle-upon-Tyne* (1812), a comprehensive and useful account of the Wall. **Hodgson's Newcastle.**

The fourth volume of the *Magna Britannia* of the Messrs. Lysons (1816), contains an article on the Roman Wall from the pen of Dr. Bennet, Bishop of Cloyne; and a good account of the Roman Inscriptions of Cumberland. **Lysons.**

The Rev. John Hodgson, M.R.S.L., devoted nearly the whole of the last volume which he lived to publish of his *History of Northumberland* to the Walls of Hadrian and Antoninus. This volume was also published separately, under the title of *The Roman Wall and South Tindale, in the* **Hodgson's Northumberland.**

Counties of Northumberland and Cumberland, 1841. This work, as well as Horsley's *Britannia Romana*, is indispensable to all who wish to study the subject thoroughly.

Abbat. *A History of the Picts' or Romano-British Wall*, by Richard Abbat, Esq., one of the author's brother-pilgrims along the line of the Roman Wall, in June, 1849.

Bruce's *Roman Wall*, first edition, 1851.

Bruce's *Roman Wall*, second edition, 1853.

C. R. Smith. In the *Collectanea Antiqua*, Vols. II. and III., Mr. Charles Roach Smith gives a graphic account of the journeys he made to different parts of the Barrier, some of them in the company of the author.

In *Once a Week*, for July and September, 1861, are some interesting papers, entitled "An Artist's Ramble along the line of the Picts' Wall," by J. W. Archer. These papers are well illustrated.

Survey of the Wall. To the munificence of His Grace the Duke of Northumberland, antiquaries are indebted for two works of the greatest importance—*A Survey of the Watling Street from the Tees to the Scotch Border*, made in the years 1850 and 1851,* and *A Survey of the Roman Wall*, made in the years 1852—1854. Mr. Henry McLauchlan, to whom the responsible task was committed, has performed it with great skill and the most scrupulous fidelity. Whoever possesses the *Survey of the Wall*, and its accompanying *Memoir*, may not only prepare advantageously for his pilgrimage, but when it is over, can easily retrace upon its accurately engraved plans, every step of his journey.

* Published by the Archæological Institute, by His Grace's generous permission, on the occasion of their Congress at Newcastle.

II.—Historical Data.

Julius Cæsar landed in Britain B.C. 55. The legions which he brought on this occasion were the seventh and the tenth. He withdrew the same year. The next summer he made a second descent, bringing five legions with him. One of these legions, the seventh, is specified by Cæsar; the others are not. This army was likewise withdrawn before the approach of winter. Julius Cæsar

The Emperor Claudius visited the island in person, having previously sent over, A.D. 43, a considerable army, consisting of the second, the ninth, the fourteenth, and the twentieth legions, together with a proper proportion of auxiliary troops. Most of these legions had an important part to perform in the history of Roman Britain. The second continued in the island until it was finally abandoned by the Romans. The ninth was surprised and nearly cut to pieces by Boadicea, and afterwards, when in Scotland, under the command of Agricola, it met with a similar misfortune. A slab found in York in 1854, commemorating the erection of a building in the reign of Trajan, by the ninth legion, furnishes us with probably the last trace of them. Horsley conjectures that the remains of this legion were incorporated with the sixth legion, which Hadrian brought over with him. The fourteenth legion was recalled by Nero; it was sent back again to Britain by Vitellius, and finally withdrawn in the reign of Vespasian. The twentieth must have remained until nearly the close of the period of Roman occupation. It had the city of Chester, the Deva of the Romans, for its head quarters. Claudius. The legions.

Caractacus.

It was in the year 50 that Caractacus and his family fell into the hands of Ostorius Scapula, Claudius' Proprætor in Britain; they were heavily ironed and sent to Rome.

Boadicea.

In the reign of Nero, A.D. 61, when Suetonius Paulinus, the Roman general, was upon an expedition in Anglesea, the Britons, commanded by Boadicea, arose and destroyed the Roman colonies.

Agricola.

By command of the Emperor Vespasian, Julius Agricola repaired to Britain as commander-in-chief. On his arrival, late in the summer, A.D. 78, he subdued the Ordovices, and reduced the Isle of Anglesea. The next year he brought into subjection the inhabitants of the lower peninsula of Britain. The year 80 saw him ravaging the country as far north as the Firth of Tay. The year 81 he spent in securing his conquest, especially by the establishment of forts in the district of the Upper Isthmus. Having done this, he overran the country northwards; and in A.D. 84 he gave battle to 30,000 Caledonians under Galgacus. Shortly after this, from motives of jealousy, he was recalled by Domitian, who, on the death of Titus, had assumed the purple.

His forts.

Battle of the Grampians.

Hadrian.

During the reigns of Nerva and Trajan we hear little of Britain. Hadrian became Emperor in the year 117; and in 120, in consequence of the turbulent state of the island, visited it in person. It was on this occasion that the sixth legion, which had previously been stationed in Germany, came to our shores. (Horsley, p. 79.) It remained here until nearly the close of the period of Roman occupation, having York for its head quarters.

The Wall.

To this period the Wall of Hadrian must be referred.

The Emperor did not remain in the country long enough to see the works complete; but he left behind him Aulus Platorius Nepos as his legate and proprætor, under whom they were carried forward.

Antoninus Pius.

Antoninus Pius succeeded Hadrian A.D. 138. During his reign the Barrier extending between the Firth of Forth and the Firth of Clyde was reared; the management of the work was committed to Lollius Urbicus, Imperial Legate and Proprætor.

M. Aur. Antoninus.

Calpurnius Agricola.

Commodus.

Ulpius Marcellus.

Whilst Marcus Aurelius Antoninus, styled the "Philosopher," held the reins of government, Britain was in a turbulent state; Calpurnius Agricola, of whom some memorials remain in the inscribed stones of the Wall, with difficulty repressed the excited passions of the people. In the reign of Commodus, the son of Marcus Aurelius, the warlike tribes burst into open insurrection. Dion Cassius gives us the following account of the affair:—"Commodus was also engaged in several wars with the barbarians . . The Britannic war, however, was the greatest of these. For some of the nations within that island having passed over the wall which divided them from the Roman stations, and, besides killing a certain commander, with his soldiers, having committed much other devastation, Commodus became alarmed, and sent Marcellus Ulpius against them." (*Monumenta Historica Britannica, p. lix.*) The Wall, its guard chambers, and stations, bear to this hour extensive marks of devastations which were committed, as is supposed, at this period. The name of Ulpius appears upon the fragment of a stone at Chesters, the ancient Cilurnum. Other legates —Perennis, Pertinax, Albinus, and Junius Severus, came in succession to Britain, during the reign of Commodus; but their efforts were not successful in establishing permanent peace, or even in preventing occasional seditious and insurrectionary movements in the army itself.

Severus.

Commodus died A.D. 192. When Lucius Septimius Severus found himself, A.D. 197, firmly established on the throne, he turned his attention to the state of Britain. His legates being unable either to purchase peace or compel the submission of the natives, he came over in person in the year 208, bringing with him his sons, Caracalla and Geta. He spent some time in making preparations. He gathered his troops from all quarters; improved the roads, restored the ruined stations, and repaired the Wall. At length, A.D. 209, all being ready, he advanced against the Caledonians. He spent three years in his enterprise, and lost fifty thousand men. Worn out with disease and vexation, he returned to York to die. His body was removed with much ceremony to Rome. His two sons, Caracalla and Geta succeeded him A.D. 211; but in the year following, the younger fell a victim to his brother's ambition.

The Caledonian Conquest.

Severus died

Geta murdered.

Caracalla.

A.D. 217, Caracalla was assasinated, when Opilius Macrinus was declared Emperor; to be assassinated in his turn, next year.

Elagabalus.

A.D. 218, Marcus Aurelius Antoninus, commonly called Elagabalus (of whom there are some lapidarian memorials in Britain), was proclaimed Emperor.

Severus Alexander.

In the year 222 Elagabalus was slain, and Severus Alexander became Emperor. Severus Alexander's assassination took place in the year 235.

Maximinus, who succeeded him, met with the usual fate of emperors, A.D. 235. Gordian (III.) became Emperor in 238, and was slain A.D. 244. Marcus Julius Philippus was next chosen Emperor; and he associated with himself in the management of the Empire his son Philip. On their assassination, A.D. 249, Quintus Trajanus Decius was proclaimed Emperor, and died two years afterwards.

Gordian and others.

Trebonianus Gallus became Emperor A.D. 251; and in the year following, associated his son Volusianus with him in the Empire.

Publius Licinius Valerianus and his son Gallienus became joint Emperors A.D. 254.

In the year 260, Gallienus became sole Emperor. During his reign a large number of usurpers arose, who are commonly denominated the "Thirty Tyrants;" of these Victorinus, Postumus, the two Tetrici, and Marius, are supposed to have been acknowledged in Britain, as their coins are frequently dug up here. M. Aurelius Claudius became Emperor A.D. 268; L. Domitius Aurelianus A.D. 270; M. Claudius Tacitus A.D. 275; M. Annius Florianus A.D. 276, (he reigned only 88 days); Aurelius Probus A.D. 276; M. Aurelius Carus A.D. 282, (who associated his sons, Carinus and Numerianus with him as Cæsars); and Aurelius Diocletianus A.D. 284. Diocletian associated with himself in the Empire M. Aur. Valer. Maximianus.

The Thirty Tyrants.

In A.D. 287, Carausius, who had charge of a fleet to repress piracy in the English Channel, revolted, and assumed the sovereignty of Britain, which he retained until A.D. 293, when he was treacherously slain by Allectus, who assumed

A British Admiral.

the government of the island. In A.D. 296, Constantius Chlorus repaired to Britain, slew Allectus, and recovered the island to its allegiance. Constantius and Galerius, who had for some years acted as subordinate Emperors or Cæsars, obtained the sovereign authority A.D. 305. In the following year Constantius died at York; and his son Constantinus, afterwards surnamed the Great, obtained the purple. In the same year (306), Maxentius, sôn of Maximianus, was proclaimed Emperor at Rome.

Constantine.

Transference of Empire.

In the year 330, Constantine transferred the seat of empire to Byzantium, which henceforth took the name of Constantinople. Constantine died A.D. 337; and his three sons, Constantinus, Constantius, and Constans were proclaimed Emperors. Magnentius, whose father was a Briton, claimed, A.D. 350, the imperial purple; but he died by his own hands the following year. Julian, called the Apostate, became Emperor A.D. 361; and was succeeded by Florus Jovianus, A.D. 363. Flavius Valentinianus assumed the purple A.D. 364; and took his brother Valens as a colleague; he afterwards further associated with himself his sons, Gratianus and Valentinianus the younger. At this period Britain was in a deplorable state; Picts, Saxons, and Scots, made it the object of incessant attacks. Gratian having become, A.D. 379, by the death of his colleagues, sole Emperor, he chose as his partner in the Empire, Theodosius, afterwards styled the Great. In the year 383, Theodosius shared the Empire with his son Arcadius. At this time Clemens Maximus, who had been sent to Britain to repel the incursions of the Picts and Scots, was proclaimed Emperor by the soldiers; in order to support his claim, he

The Picts.

passed over with his forces to the continent, draining the island of its youth.

Theodosius dying, A.D. 395, he was succeeded by his two sons, Honorius and Arcadius; Honorius being made Emperor of the West, and Arcadius of the East. Honorius.

In the year 396, the Britons sent ambassadors to Rome, asking for assistance. A legion is said to have been sent to them, by command of Stilicho, and their enemies were for a time repressed. Stilicho.

A.D. 407, This was a season of intestine tumult in Britain. The soldiers successively invested Marcus, Gratian, and Constantine, with the purple. Constantine transferred his army to Gaul, and made a successful stand against Honorius.

A.D. 410, Honorius, harassed by the Goths and other enemies, wrote to the Britons informing them he was no longer able to help them, and that they must look to themselves for safety. The poor Britons.

A.D. 418, *The Saxon Chronicle* says, "This year the Romans collected all the treasures that were in Britain; and some they hid in the earth, so that no one has since been able to find them; and some they carried with them into Gaul."

A.D. 446, Britain was abandoned by the Romans.—*Horsley*.

III.—Military Data.

The Notitia.

A document has come down to our times from the Roman age, which is of great use in elucidating the arrangements of the Wall. It is entitled *Notitia Dignitatum et Administrationum omnium tam civilium quam militarium in partibus orientis et occidentis*," and, contains an account of the disposal of the chief dignitaries of the Empire, civil and military, throughout the world. The following is the portion of it which relates to the Wall; the section is headed *"Item per lineam Valli"*—also along the line of the Wall.

Stations and troops along the line of Wall.

The Tribune of the fourth cohort of the Lingones at Segedunum.
The Tribune of the cohort of the Cornovii at Pons Ælii.
The Prefect of the first ala, or wing, of the Astures at Condercum.
The Tribune of the first cohort of the Frixagi (Frisii) at Vindobala.
The Prefect of the Savinian ala at Hunnum.
The Prefect of the second ala of Astures at Cilurnum.
The Tribune of the first cohort of the Batavians at Procolitia.
The Tribune of the first cohort of the Tungri at Borcovicus.
The Tribune of the fourth cohort of the Gauls at Vindolana.
The Tribune of the first cohort of the Astures at Æsica.
The Tribune of the second cohort of the Dalmatians at Magna.
The Tribune of the first cohort of Dacians, styled "Ælia," at Amboglanna.
The Prefect of the ala, called "Petriana," at Petriana.
The Prefect of a detachment of Moors, styled "Aureliani," at Aballaba.
The Tribune of the second cohort of the Lergi at Congavata.
The Tribune of the first cohort of the Spaniards at Axelodunum.
The Tribune of the second cohort of the Thracians at Gabrosentum.
The Tribune of the first marine cohort, styled "Ælia," at Tunnocelum.
The Tribune of the first cohort of the Morini at Glannibanta.
The Tribune of the third cohort of the Nervii at Alionis.
The Cuneus of men in armour at Bremetenracum.
The Prefect of the first ala, styled Herculean, at Olenacum.
The Tribune of the sixth cohort of the Nervii at Virosidum

The precise period when the *Notitia* was compiled is not known. It was probably written about the beginning of fifth century, and certainly before the abandonment of Britain by the Romans. By it the names of the stations are ascertained. Thus, for example, when in a camp, now called Housesteads, many altars are found bearing the name of the first cohort of the Tungri, and when, on referring to the *No-*

titia, we find that the commander of the first cohort of the Tungri was stationed at Borcovicus, the inference becomes strong that Housesteads is the Borcovicus of the Romans; and this probability becomes a moral certainty, when the stations on either side of it yield tablets inscribed with the names of the first cohort of the Batavians, and the fourth cohort of the Gauls, the troops which the *Notitia* places in the stations immediately to the east and west of Borcovicus. The Stations ascertained.

Antonine's Itinerary.

The *Itinerary* of Antonine is another work of much importance in settling the Roman stations in Britain and other countries. It gives the routes pursued by the soldiers in their marches, the stations at which they halted, and the distance between them in Roman miles. It is usually ascribed to the reign of Caracalla. The Itinerary.

The Army, and its Officers.

The Legion was the main division of a Roman army. At first none of the lower class were admitted into the army; afterwards, the legion was composed of any one having the rank of a Roman citizen. In early times, the legion consisted of about 4000 foot soldiers; in the time of Hadrian, its complement was 6000. The Legion.

Each legion had a troop of 300 or 400 horse soldiers attached to it. Originally the cavalry consisted entirely of *equites*, knights; in later times foreign troops were used for this purpose, and hence they were regarded as auxiliaries simply, and as not belonging to the legion. As the cavalry generally formed the wing of an army, a troop of horse was termed an *Ala*. Attached to each legion, was a number of Cavalry. Alæ.

troops (besides the cavalry) called auxiliaries. In later times the Roman army chiefly consisted of these.

Cohorts.

Each legion was divided into ten cohorts, each Cohort into three maniples, and each Maniple into two centuries. Each Century consisted, when complete, as its name implies, of 100 men.

Officers.

The principal officers in the legion were Tribunes, of which there were six to each legion. Each century was commanded by a Centurion. Each centurion had under him two officers, acting as lieutenants, called *Optiones*, and two *Signiferi* or standard-bearers. The term *Vexillarius* was also applied to the bearer of the standard (*vexillum*). In inscriptions found on the Wall, the term *Vexillatio* is occasionally met with; it is supposed to refer either to a body of *Vexillarii* (veteran soldiers), or any body of soldiers united under one flag; it is applied to both horse and foot soldiers.

Each *Ala* or troop of horse (about 300 in number), was divided into ten squadrons called *Turmæ*, and each *Turma* into three *Decuriæ* (consisting usually of ten men). The *Decuria* was commanded by a Decurion. A Prefect (equivalent in rank to the Tribune of the legion) commanded the whole *ala*. The term *Numerus* occurs in the *Notitia*, and in inscriptions. It seems to be a general term, similar to our word band or troop. It is most frequently applied to cavalry, though not exclusively.

Superior officers.

Mention is made in inscriptions of officers of a superior class to any of those already named. The Proconsuls and Propraetors were the governors of the Province. The office of Consul was in its origin essentially of a military nature, and that of Prætor of a judicial or civil character. When a province was in a state of revolt, the command of it was conferred upon a Proconsul, but when the developement of its internal resources was the object of most importance, a Proprætor was appointed; this distinction, however, was not always observed. The Legate was a military officer, not attached to any particular corps, but exercising a general superintendence of a country, under the provincial governor. His rank corresponded to that of a lieutenant-general in a modern army. The following terms are also met with:— Military terms.

Emeriti, soldiers who had served their full time; *Evocati*, veterans again called out as volunteers—the Emperor's body-guard; *Ex-evocati*, veterans a second time discharged; *Beneficiarii*, soldiers who had received some honour, or special exemption from the drudgeries of service; *Duplares*, soldiers receiving double pay as a reward.

IV.—Height above the Level of the Sea of the Principal Points of the Wall.

These are taken from Mr. McLauchlan's *Memoir*, and though no doubt very nearly accurate, profess to be approximations to the truth only.

Benwell	.. .. *feet* 380	Housesteads	.. .. *feet* 730	
Chapel Hill	 400	Barcombe Stone	.. 800	
Rutchester	 410	Chesterholm	 560	
Harlow Hill	 460	Winshields	 1000	Summit
Down Hill	 670	Great Chesters	.. 550	
Halton Chesters	.. 600	Walltown Crags	.. 860	
Wall 1½ m. west of Halton	800	Carvoran	 530	
St. Oswalds	 730	Birdoswald	 600	
Limestone Corner	.. 800	Bankshead	 480	
Carrawburgh	 650	Hare Hill	.. . 350	
Carraw House	 770	Cambeck Fort	 220	
Sewingshields	 960	Newtown	 300	

CHAPTER II.

A GENERAL VIEW OF THE WORKS.

Intention of the Wall.

The Roman Wall, or as it used to be called, the Picts' Wall, is a great fortification intended to act not only as a fence against a northern enemy, but to be used as the basis of military operations against a foe on either side of it.

It cannot have been reared as the northern limit of the Roman Empire; for (1) every station and every mile castle along its course seems to have been provided with a wide portal, opening towards the north; and (2) there are some stations situated far to the north of the Wall, on the line both of the Watling Street and of the Maiden Way, which can be proved to have been garrisoned by Roman troops until near the close of the period of Roman occupation in Britain.

This great fortification consists of three parts:—

Its parts.

1. A Stone Wall, with a ditch on its northern side. 2. An Earth Wall or Vallum, south of the stone wall. 3. Stations, Castles, Watch-towers, and Roads, for the accommodation of the soldiery who manned the Wall, and for the transmission of military stores. These lie, for the most part, between the stone wall and the earthen lines.

Relation of the Wall and Vallum.

The whole of the works proceed from one side of the island to the other in a nearly direct line, and in comparatively close companionship. The stone wall and earthern rampart are generally within sixty or eighty yards of each other. The distance between them, however, varies according to the nature of the country. In one instance they approach within thirty yards of each other, while in another, they are half a mile apart. It is in the high grounds of the central region that they are most widely separated. Midway between the seas, the country attains a considerable elevation; here the stone wall seeks the highest ridges, but the Vallum, forsaking for a while its usual companion, runs along the adjacent valley. Both works are however so arranged as to afford each other the greatest amount of support which the nature of the country allows. The Wall usually seizes those positions which give it the greatest advantage on its northern margin; the Vallum on the other hand, has been drawn with the view of occupying ground that is strongest towards the south.

The stone Wall extends from Wallsend on the Tyne to Bowness on the Solway, a distance of about seventy-three English miles and a half. (McLauchlan's *Memoir*, p. 5.) The earth wall falls short of this distance by about three miles at each end; not extending beyond Newcastle on the east side, and Dykesfield on the west.

Length of Wall.

Most writers who have treated of the Roman remains in Britain, have considered that the various parts of the fortification are the work of different periods.

Horsley conceived that the stations and the north agger of the Vallum were the work of Agricola; that the southern mounds and fosse of the Vallum were the work of Hadrian; and that the stone Wall was reared by Severus. Other writers maintain that the stone Wall was erected by Theodosius and Honorius, about the close of the fourth and the beginning of the fifth century.

One work. In all probability, the whole series of fortifications were the work of one period, and were reared at the command of Hadrian. Deferring the discussion of this question until the works have been examined in detail, it will meanwhile be convenient to speak of the whole series as being but different parts of one great engineering scheme.

The most striking feature in the plan, both of the Murus and the Vallum, is the determinate manner in which they pursue their straightforward course. The Vallum makes fewer deviations from a right line than the stone Wall; * but as the Wall traverses higher ground, this remarkable tendency is more easily detected in it than in the other. Shooting over the country, in its onward course, it only swerves from a straight line to take in its route the boldest elevations. So far from declining a hill, it usually selects one. For nineteen miles out of Newcastle the road to Carlisle runs upon the foundation of the Wall, and during the summer months its dusty surface contrasts well with the surrounding verdure. Often will the traveller, after attaining some of the steep acclivities of his path, observe the road stretching for miles in an undeviating course to the east and to the west of him, resembling, as Hutton expresses it, a

* This peculiarity of the Vallum has been strikingly brought out in Mr. McLauchlan's Survey. West of Harlow Hill it runs for nearly five miles in a straight line. West of Limestone Corner in runs in the direction of Sewingshields Crags three miles and a half without bending. Between Banks-hill and Sandysike, a distance of three miles and a half, it pursues a direct course.—*Memoir*, pp. 18, 34, 61.

white ribbon on a green ground. But if the Wall seldom deviates from a right line, except to occupy the highest points, it never fails to seize them, as they occur, no matter how often it is compelled, with this view, to change its direction. This mode of proceeding involves another peculiarity. The Wall is compelled to accomodate itself to the depressions of the mountainous region over which it passes. Without flinching, it sinks into the "gap," or pass, which ever and anon occurs, and, having crossed the narrow valley, ascends unfalteringly the acclivity on the other side. The antiquary, in following the Wall into these ravines, is often compelled to step with the utmost caution, and in clambering up the opposite ascent, he is as frequently constrained to pause for breath.

I.—The Wall.

In no part of its course is the Wall entirely perfect, and therefore it is difficult to ascertain what its original height has been. Bede, whose cherished home was the monastery of Jarrow, anciently part of the parish of Wallsend, is the earliest author who gives its dimensions. He says, "It is eight feet in breadth, and twelve in height, in a straight line from east to west, as is still visible to beholders."

Its dimensions.

Subsequent writers assign to it a greater elevation. Sir Christopher Ridley, writing about the year 1572, gives it the following dimensions:—"The bredth iij yardis, the hyght remaneth in sum placis yet vij yardis." Samson Erdeswick, an English antiquary of some celebrity, visited the Wall, in the year 1574. His account is:—"As towching Hadrian's Wall, begyning abowt a town called Bonus standing vppon the river Sulway now called Eden, and there yet standing of the heyth of 16 fote, for almost a quarter of a myle together, and so along the river syde estwards." Camden, who visited the Wall in 1599, says—"Within two furlongs of Carvoran, on a pretty high hill, the Wall is still standing, fifteen feet in height, and nine in breadth." These statements leave upon the mind an impression that the estimate of Bede is too low. In all probability, the Wall would be surmounted by a battlement of not less than four feet in height, and as this part of the structure would be the first to fall into decay, Bede's calculation was probably irrespective of it. This, however, only gives us a total elevation of sixteen feet. Unless we reject the evidence of Ridley and Erdeswick, we must admit, even after making due allowance for error and exaggeration, that the Wall, when in its integrity, was, in some parts of its course, eighteen or nineteen feet high. This elevation would be in keeping with its breadth.

The thickness of the Wall varies considerably; in some places it is six feet, in others nine feet and a half. Probably the prevailing width is eight feet, the measurement given by Bede.

The frequency with which the thickness of the Wall varies favours the idea that numerous gangs of labourers were simultaneously employed upon the work, and that each superintending centurion was allowed to use his discretion as to its width. The northern face of the Wall is continuous, but the southern has numerous outsets and insets, measuring from four to twelve inches at the points where the sections of the different companies joined.

The Fosse.

Throughout the whole of its length, the Wall was accompanied on its northern margin by a broad and deep Fosse, which, by increasing the comparative height of the Wall, added greatly to its strength. This portion of the Barrier may yet be traced, with trifling interruptions, from sea to sea. Even in places where the Wall has quite disappeared, its more lowly companion, the fosse, remains.

When the ditch traverses a flat or exposed country, a portion of the materials taken out of it has frequently been thrown upon its northern margin, so as to present to the enemy an additional rampart. In those positions, on the other hand, where its assistance could be of no avail, as along the edge of a cliff, the fosse does not appear.

No small amount of labour has been expended in the excavation of the ditch; it has been drawn indifferently through alluvial soil, and rocks of sandstone, limestone, and basalt. The great labour which this involved is well seen at the top of Limestone Bank, where enormous blocks of whinstone lie just as they have been lifted out of the fosse. The fosse never leaves the Wall to avoid a mechanical difficulty.

The size of the ditch in several places is still considerable. To the east of Heddon-on-the-Wall, it measures thirty-four feet across the top, and is nearly nine feet deep; as it descends the hill from Carvoran to Thirlwall, it measures forty feet across the top, fourteen across the bottom, and is ten feet deep. To the west of Limestone Corner is a portion which, reckoning from the top of the supplemental mound on its northern margin, has a depth of twenty feet. The dimensions of the fosse were probably not uniform throughout the line; but these examples prepare us to receive, as tolerably correct, Hutton's estimate of its average size. "The ditch to the north was as near as convenient, thirty-six feet wide and fifteen feet deep."

II.—The Vallum.

Its parts. The Vallum or Earth Wall, is uniformly to the south of the stone Wall. It consists of three ramparts and a fosse. One of these ramparts is placed close upon the southern edge of the ditch, the two others of larger dimensions stand, one to the north, and the other to the south of it, at the distance of about twenty-four feet. The annexed section of the works near the 18th mile-stone west of New- (Section.)

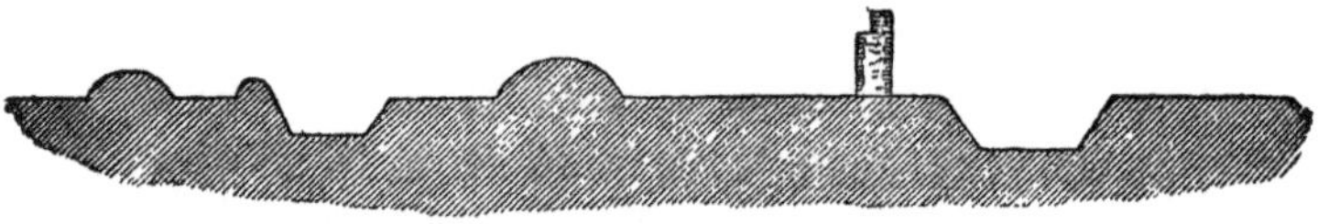

castle exhibits their present condition. It is drawn to the scale of seventy-five feet to the inch. The Wall itself, though shown in the cut is, unhappily, entirely removed.

Dimensions. The ramparts, in some parts of the line, stand, even at present, six or seven feet above the level of the neighbouring ground. They are composed of earth, mingled, not unfrequently, with masses of stone. Occasionally, the stone preponderates to such an extent as to yield to the hand of the modern spoiler ready materials for the formation of stone dikes. In several places they are being quarried with this view.

The fosse of the Vallum is of a character similar to the fosse of the stone Wall; but, judging from present appearances, its dimensions have been rather less. It, too, has been frequently cut through beds of stone.

Although the distance between the stone Wall and the Vallum is, as already observed, perpetually varying, the lines of the Vallum maintain amongst themselves nearly the same relative position throughout their entire course.

No apparent paths of egress have been made through these southern lines of fortification. The only mode of communication with the country to the south originally contemplated seems to have been by the gateways of the stations.

If we adopt the theory that the Wall and the Vallum exhibit unity of design, a question of some importance arises—With what view was the Vallum constructed? The true answer to this inquiry seems to have been hit upon even before Horsley's time. That able antiquary, referring to the relative position of the Wall and the Vallum, says—"Such considerations as these have induced some to believe that what now goes by the name of Hadrian's work was originally designed for a fence against any sudden insurrection of the provincial Britons, and particularly of the Brigantes" (p. 125). A careful examination of the country over which the Wall runs, and the fact which Horsley thus states —"That the southern prospect of Hadrian's work, and the defence on that side, is generally better than on the north; whereas the northern prospect and defence have been principally or only taken care of in the Wall of Severus," almost necessarily lead to the conclusion, that whilst the

Its use.

Wall undertook the harder duty of warding off the professedly hostile tribes of Caledonia, the Vallum was intended as a protection against sudden surprise from the south. The natives of the country on the south side of the Wall, though conquered, were not to be depended upon; in the event of their kinsmen in the north gaining an advantage, they would be ready to avail themselves of it. The Romans knew this, and with characteristic prudence made themselves secure on both sides.

III.—Stations and Roads.

The third, and perhaps the most important part of the fortification, consisted of the structures that were formed for the accommodation of the soldiery, and for the ready transmission of troops and stores. Neither stone walls, nor ditches, nor earthen ramparts, would alone have proved material impediments to the incursions of the Caledonians—

> "An iron race, . . .
> Foes to the gentler genius of the plain."

It is reported that Agesilaus, when asked where were the walls of Sparta, pointed to his soldiers and said "There." The Romans placed their chief reliance on the valour and discipline of their armies, though they did not despise the assistance of mural lines. In a foreign country, to which it was difficult to transmit relays of troops, it became a matter of great importance to economise the lives of the soldiery. Hence arose the Wall.

Those portions of the Wall which yet await our consideration, are the Stations, Mile-castles, Turrets, and Roads.

At distances along the line which average nearly four miles, Stationary Camps (*stationes* or *castra stativa*) were erected. These received their distinctive appellation in contradistinction to those temporary camps which were thrown up when an army halted for a night or some brief period. Stations.

The stations on the line of the Wall were military cities, suited to be the residence of the chief who commanded the district, and providing secure lodgement for the powerful body of soldiery he had under him.

Some of the stations, though connected with the Wall, have evidently been built before it. This is shown by the north wall of the station being independent of the great Wall. To secure a safe retreat for the soldiers employed upon the work, would necessarily be the first care of the builder.

The stations are quadrangular in their form, though rounded at the corners, and contain an area of from three to five acres. The station of Birdoswald, which is the largest, contains five and a half acres. Drumburgh contains only three-quarters of an acre, but this is an extreme case. A stone wall, about five feet thick, incloses them, and has probably in every instance been strengthened by a fosse; and occasionally an earthen rampart is added. They usually stand upon ground which slopes to the south, and is naturally defended upon one side at least.

The Wall, when it does not fall in with the northern wall of a station, usually comes up to the northern cheek of its eastern and western gateways. The Vallum, in like manner, usually approaches close to the southern wall of the station, or comes up to the defence of the southern side of the eastern and western portals. At least three of the stations, it must, however, be observed, are quite detached from both lines of fortification, being situated to the south of them. They probably belonged to Agricola's series of forts.

All the stations have, on their erection, been provided, after the usual method of Roman castrametation, with at least four gateways; in several instances one or more of these portals have been walled up at some period prior to the final abandonment of the fortification.

Streets.

In some of the best preserved stations the main streets proceeding from the four gateways, and crossing each other at right angles, may be discovered. The minor streets which communicated with these were very narrow, but parallel to the main ones. The remains of suburbs, for the accommodation, probably, of the camp followers, have been found outside the walls of most of the great camps.

In selecting a spot for a station, care has been taken that a copious supply of water should be at hand. The springs, rivulets, wells, and aqueducts, whence they procured the needful fluid, are still, in many places, to be traced.

The stations, as we might expect on an enemy's frontier, have been constructed with a view to security, not luxury or display. In this respect they show a striking contrast with the Roman buildings in the south of England. No traces of a tesselated pavement have been found in the mural region; the nearest approach to it being some lozenge-shaped flooring tiles at Birdoswald.

For the most part, the stations now present a scene of utter desolation. The wayfarer may pass through them without knowing it. The sheep, depasturing the grass-grown ruins, look listlessly upon the passer-by, and the curlew, wheeling above his head, screams as at the presence of an intruder. Whether or not sites naturally fertile were chosen for the stations does not appear; but certain it is, that they are now, for the most part, coated with a sward more green and more luxuriant than that which covers the contiguous grounds. Centuries of occupation have given them a degree of fertility which, probably, they will never lose. One can scarcely turn up the soil without meeting, not only with fragments of Roman pottery and other imperishable articles, but with the bones of oxen, the tusks of boars, the horns of deer, and other animal remains.

Names of the stations.

It is not a little remarkable that the names of the stations, which must have been household words in the days of Roman occupation, have for the most part been obliterated from the local vocabulary. The truth is, that military reasons dictated the choice of the stations,—commercial facilities give rise to modern cities.

The number of stations given in the *Notitia* list, as being situated *per lineam Valli*, is twenty-three. Horsley conceived that eighteen of these were immediately connected with the Wall, and that the rest were supporting stations to the north and the south of it. This opinion is probably near the truth, but as the stations following Amboglanna towards the west have not been ascertained with certainty, some doubt must remain upon it.

Mile Castles.

In addition to the stations, Castella or Mile-Castles were provided for the use of the troops which garrisoned the Wall. They derive their modern name from the circumstance of their being usually placed at the distance of a

Roman mile from each other. They were quadrangular buildings, differing somewhat in size, but usually measuring about sixty feet from east to west, and fifty from north to south. They have evidently been built at the same time as the Wall; their walls being of the same kind of masonry as the Wall, and of the same thickness. They are placed immediately within the Wall, that structure forming their north wall. Though generally placed at about seven furlongs, or a Roman mile, from each other, the nature of the ground, independently of distance, has frequently determined the spot of their location. Whenever the Wall has had occasion to traverse a river or a mountain-pass, a mile-castle has usually been placed on the one side or other to guard the defile. Judging from the most perfect specimens which remain, these mile-towers have been provided with wide portals of massive masonry in the centre of their northern and southern sides. Their southern angles have been rounded off on the outside. It is not easy to conjecture what were the internal arrangements of these buildings; probably they afforded little accommodation beyond what their four strong walls and well-barred gates gave. It is not unlikely that temporary structures were placed within them, with roofs leaning against the walls of the main building. The foundations of such structures have been found in several of them.

Turrets

Between the mile-castles, four subsidiary buildings, generally denominated Turrets or Watch Towers, were placed. They were little more than stone sentry-boxes. Horsley, in his day, complained that "scarce three of them could be made out in succession." Scarcely one along the whole line can now with certainty be determined. They contained an interior space of eight or ten feet square. Horsley reckons that there must have been three hundred and twenty of them in all. Though small buildings, they were, like all the works of the Romans, built for perpetuity. The remnants of the walls of one near Birdoswald are three feet thick.

But all these arrangements were not enough; without Roads, one important element in the strength of the Great Barrier would be wanting. Nothing economizes military force more effectually than the possession of means for quickly concentrating all available resources upon any point which the enemy may select for attack. The advance of Roman armies, and the formation of roads, were uniformly contemporaneous. The mural fortress therefore had its Military Way. Without it all the rest would have been useless. It would not perhaps be incorrect to say, that both Vallum and Wall were subsidiary to it, and that the chief use of these structures was to guard the road, and to protect and conceal from view, both on the north and south, the troops that marched along it. Roads.

The Military Way is usually about twenty feet wide. It is composed of rubble stone, chiefly trap. Its surface is rounded, the centre being elevated a foot or eighteen inches above the adjoining ground. The mode of its formation seems to have been this:—a couple of stones were placed endwise in the centre; others were placed on each side of these, slightly leaning upon them, and when the proper width was attained, stout kerb-stones defined each margin and perfected the work. By this means the pressure was distributed over the whole surface. When carried along the slope of a hill, the hanging side of the road was made up by unusually large kerb stones. In most places where the way still remains, it is completely grass-grown, but may, notwithstanding, be easily distinguished from the neighbouring ground by the colour of its herbage; the dryness of its substratum allowing the growth of a finer description of plant. For the same reason, a sheep-track generally runs along it. For the accommodation of the soldiery, the road went from castle to castle, and so, from station to station. In doing this it did not always keep close to the Wall, but took the easiest path between the required points. In traversing the precipitous grounds between Sewingshields and Thirlwall, the ingenuity of the engineer has been severely tried; but most successfully has he performed his task. Whilst, as previously observed, the Wall shoots over the highest and steepest summits, the road pursues its tortuous course from one platform of the rock to another, so as to bring the traveller from mile-castle to mile-castle by the easiest possible gradients.

Direct road.

Besides the road now described, which throughout its entire length keeps within the two great lines of fortification, another, situated to the south of both Murus and Vallum, has afforded direct communication between some of the stations. From Cilurnum to Magna, the Wall forms a curved line, in order to gain the highest hills of the district. For the accommodation of those whose business did not require them to call at any intermediate point, a road went, like the string of a bow, direct from the one station to the other. This road passes near the modern village of Newburgh, and skirts the north gate of the station at

Chesterholm, near to which a Roman mile-stone still stands.

In estimating the resources of this great fortification, we must also bear in mind that two great lines of communication—the Watling Street and the Maiden Way—intersected the country from north to south, and that many subsidiary roads bore down upon them. The sixth legion, whose head-quarters were at York, would have no difficulty, at any season of the year, in coming to the aid of the auxiliaries to whom the defence of the Wall was more immediately intrusted.

Speaking tubes.

If tradition is to be credited, the Romans were not satisfied with roads as a means of rapidly communicating information; speaking-trumpets or pipes, we are told, ran along the whole length of the Wall. It may perhaps be sufficient to say that no one is known to have seen these speaking-tubes; though earthen and lead pipes, for the conveyance of water, are not unfrequently met with in the stations.

Masonry.

The Masonry of the Wall next demands attention. The stones employed in building the Wall and stations were very carefully selected. When good stones were to be had near at hand, they were taken; but those of inferior quality were never used to avoid the labour of bringing better from a distance. In some parts of the line, in Cumberland especially, the stone must have been brought from quarries seven or eight miles off. A quartzose grit was generally selected, not only on account of its hardness, but because its rough surface gave it a firmer adhesion to the mortar.

Quarries.

The quarries from which the stone has been procured can, in many instances, be precisely ascertained. On Fallow-

Rock markings.

field Fell, not far from Chollerford, is an ancient quarry, on the face of which the words,

[P]ETRA FLAVI[I] CARANTINI,

The rock of Flavius Carantinus—are still to be traced.

Roman quarries.

On opening out, in the year 1837, some old quarries on the high, brown hill of Barcombe, near Thorngrafton, a small copper vessel was found, containing a large number of coins, all of the Upper Empire. North of Busy-Gap the wedge-holes yet remain in some slabs of rock that rise to the surface. A Roman quarry existed on Haltwhistle Fell, on which was formerly the inscription, LEG.VI.V. In Cumberland there are several Roman inscriptions on the face of the ancient quarries. About two miles west of Birdoswald, and little more than a quarter of a mile south of the road, is Coome Crag, on which are several Roman inscriptions, made apparently by the quarrymen. The most remarkable of this class of Antiquities, is the "Written Rock of the Gelt," near Brampton, which is here shewn.*

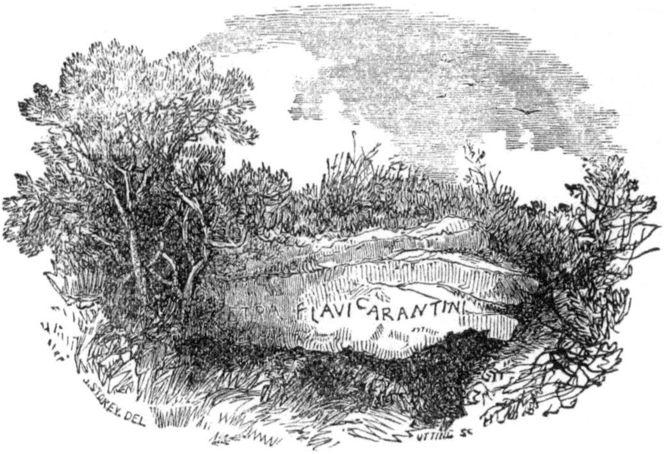

The general purport of the inscription is:—"A vexillation of the second legion, under an optio called Agricola, were, in the consulship of Flavius Aper and Albinus Maximus, A.D. 207, [employed here to hew stone.]"

The exterior masonry of the Wall consists, on both sides, of carefully squared freestone blocks; the interior, of rubble of any description firmly imbedded in mortar. The

The facing stones.

* Perhaps the best way of going to the Written Rock is the following:—Alight at the Milton station, on the railway. Take the road which leads to Brampton-Fell House. Here enquire for the Wreay Farm. Thence go to Unity. The pilgrim will here be within 400 or 500 yards of the inscription. If he cannot find it, some friendly quarryman will point it out.

character of the facing-stones is peculiar, yet tolerably uniform. They are eight or nine inches thick, and ten or eleven broad; their length, which is perhaps their characteristic feature, frequently amounts to twenty inches. The part of the stone exposed to the weather is cut across "the bait," so as to avoid its scaling off by the lines of stratification; the stone tapers towards the end which is set into the Wall, and has a form nearly resembling that of a wedge. Owing to the extent to which the stones are set into the Wall, the necessity of bonding tiles—so characteristic of Roman masonry in the south of England—is altogether superseded. Stones of the shape and size which have now been described were just those which could be most easily wrought in the quarry, most conveniently carried on the backs of the impressed Britons to the Wall, and most easily fitted into their bed. The uniformity in their appearance is such as to enable us, after a little practice, at once to recognise them in the churches, castles, farm-buildings, and fences of the district through which the Wall runs.

The accompanying illustrations, taken from Trajan's column, show the mode in which the stones were carried.

The stones of some of the stations (Cilurnum for example) are smaller than those of the Wall. The internal buildings of the stations have also been composed of small stones.

The front of the stones, both of the Wall and stations, is roughly "scabbled" with the pick. In some parts of the line, this tooling takes a definite form; when this is the case, the marking called the diamond broaching is most common. Sometimes the stone is scored with waved lines, or with small squares, or with nearly upright lines.

The tenacity of the mortar which was used forms an important element in the strength of the whole fabric. It has evidently been of a nature similar to the grout and concrete of the present day. The lime has been used fresh. It has been well mixed with a considerable quantity of sand and gravel, and an abundance of water has been added to the mixture shortly before use. Mortar thus prepared speedily hardens. The Mortar.

Occasionally, but by no means frequently, small pieces of charcoal are mixed with the mortar. These have evidently been derived from the wood used in burning the lime. Excepting in the buildings of the stations, pounded tile, so characteristic of the Roman mortar in the south of England, is not a common ingredient in the mortar of the Wall. Limestone is abundant in most parts of the district through which the Wall passes. The Romans probably burnt it in "sow kilns." The limestone and fuel being arranged in alternate layers, the whole was carefully covered with turf and ignited. This simple method is still much resorted to when lime is wanted for farm purposes.

Mode of building.

Supposing the stones to be now quarried and squared, the lime burnt and mixed with sand and gravel, the next point to be attended to is the method of using them. The foundation was prepared by the removal of the natural soil to the width of about nine feet. In the hill district, a very scanty portion of earth covers the rocks; in the richer regions an excavation of from fifteen to eighteen inches has been made before the subsoil was reached. On the outer and inner margins of the ground thus bared, two rows of flags, of from two to four inches in thickness, and from eighteen to twenty in breadth, were generally laid; no mortar was placed under them; but not unfrequently a quantity of well-puddled clay. On these was laid the first course of facing-stones, which were usually the largest stones used in the structure. In the higher courses the facing-stones are uniformly of freestone, but in the ground course a "whinstone" is occasionally introduced. The flagstones of the foundation usually project from one to five inches beyond the first course of facing-stones, and these again usally stand out an inch or two beyond the second course, after which the wall is taken straight up.

One or two courses of facing-stones having been placed in their beds and carefully pointed, a mass of mortar in a very fluid state was poured into the interior of the wall, and stones of any kind or shape that were of a convenient size were "puddled" in amongst it. Whinstones, as being most abundant in the district, are generally used for the filling. Course after course was added, and one mass of concrete imposed upon another, until the Wall reached the required height. When the whole was finished it formed a solid, compact mass, without any holes or crevices in the interior, and in a short time became as firm as unhewn rock.

In some parts of the line the mortar has been "hand-laid." The rubble of the interior having been first disposed in its place, the mortar has been laid upon it with a trowel. In this case the mortar never penetrates the interstices of the mass, and does not make such solid masonry as the method generally pursued. When, however, this plan is adopted, the rubble stones are often laid upon their edges in a slanting position, somewhat in the fashion of herring-bone masonry.

On gently waving ground the courses of the Wall follow the undulations of the surface, but on steep inclines the stones are laid parallel to the horizon.

Time in building.

It is sometimes asked, How long would the Wall be in building? From calculations that have been made, founded upon the experience gained by the construction of the vast works connected with modern railways, it is considered that, in the existing circumstances of the country at the time, the *Vallum* and the *Murus* could not be reared in a shorter period than ten years. The cost of it, in our present currency, would be about a million of pounds. Above ten thousand men would be required to garrison its stations.

Cost.

CHAPTER III.

LOCAL DESCRIPTION.

I.—Wallsend to Newcastle.

Wallsend. The village of Wallsend, once so famous for its coal, takes its name from the Roman Wall. Here was the eastern extremity of the great structure. At this point the river becomes sufficiently wide to prove of itself a strong barrier.* Here was planted the station of SEGEDVNVM, the first of those given in the *Notitia* as being *per lineam Valli*. The site of the station is good. Without being so much elevated as to give it a painful exposure to the blasts of the north and the east, it commands an extensive view in every direction. The ground in front of it has a full exposure to the mid-day sun. The station stands upon an angle of the

The river. river, formed by two of the longest "reaches" which the stream makes in the whole of its course. The "Long Reach" extends downwards as far as the high end of South Shields, and the "Bill Reach" stretches nearly two miles up the water. In both directions, therefore, any operations conducted on the river could be easily discerned by the Roman garrison. Although it was not thought requisite to extend the Wall farther along the northern bank of the

* The width of the river here has been much contracted of late. Embankments have been thrust into it to the extent of 706 feet on each side.

Tyne than Wallsend, special precautions were taken to guard the mouth of the estuary. Proofs of Roman occupation have been found on the promontory where the ruins of Tynemouth Priory now stand, and at the western extremity of North Shields; and on the southern side of the river camps have been planted at Tyne Law (opposite Tynemouth Priory) and at Jarrow.

In a neighbourhood where mining operations have, in modern times, been conducted on an extensive scale, any very marked indications of Roman occupation cannot be expected. It is satisfactory, however, to find some traces. The grass-grown mound of the eastern rampart may be still noticed, defended by its ditch. The southern rampart may also be partially detected. The rounded angle formed by the junction of these walls is tolerably distinct. The defile which formed the strength of the station on its west side has been filled up; the commencement of its dip may, however, be seen. The house occupied by Mr. Reay is just within the eastern rampart of the station, and that which was so long known as Mr. Buddle's house (now occupied by Mr. Leslie), is just within the line of what was its western rampart. The shaft of the famous Wallsend colliery is a few yards to the west of the western rampart.

The ramparts.

In order to prevent an enemy passing between the station and the river, a wall came down from the south-east angle of the station into the river. Some traces of this wall may be noticed, particularly at the point where it joins what was the margin of the river. Mr. Buddle used to say, that when bathing in the river, as a boy, he had often noticed the foundations of this wall extending far into the

The river wall.

river. Mr. Leslie has seen it as far as the lowest tides enabled him to observe. The station is supposed to have contained an area of three acres and a half.

Several swellings of the ground on the south and on the east of the station indicate the ruins of suburban buildings. Numerous proofs of Roman occupation have, at various times, been found in the station. Roman pottery and coins are frequently found. Human bones and those of the inferior animals have been dug up in considerable quantities. In excavating a cellar under the dining-room of Wallsend House, a well was found. Inscriptions. The inscribed stones which have been found at this station are not of much importance. The only one which remains on the spot is in the possession of Mr. Reay, and it bears the words LEG. II. AVG.—"The second legion, styled the August." The northern portion of the station is quite obliterated. There can be no doubt that the rampart in this direction lay to the north of the present road. The Wall in its course westward has probably proceeded from the north jamb of the western gateway, allowing the northern part of the station to project beyond it.

Wallsend Coal Pit.

Digression. A stranger to the district may wish, before leaving Wallsend, to have some information respecting its famous colliery. The Newcastle coal basin here attains its greatest depression, and at the bottom of the basin the coal is said to be always the best in quality. The pit was sunk by Messrs. William Chapman and Brothers in 1770. Before they reached the coal their finances were exhausted. They made over their rights to the Messrs. Russell and Wade of Sunderland, their bankers, in discharge of their overdrawn account. The new partners soon reached the coal. This was in 1771. The High Main seam was wrought out in 1818, and then the lower, or Bensham, seam was had recourse to. The Messrs. Russell and Co. relinquished their interest in the pit in 1847; and in 1853 (the concern having become unprofitable), it was abandoned altogether. Its workings are now full of water. The original shaft is in front of Mr. Leslie's door. A second shaft (the B pit) is also close at hand. When the colliery was in full play, two other shafts were made use of—there being four in all. The royalty belongs to the Dean and Chapter of Durham. The Messrs. Russell, during the period of their tenancy, paid the Chapter sums varying from £1000 to £4000 *per annum.* The average profit of the pit, during a period of twenty years, was £20,000 *per annum.* One year it gave the partners a clear return of £60,000. Three hundred and fifty men and boys were usually employed in the workings.*

Traces of the stone Wall are very indistinct between Wallsend and Newcastle, but its course is marked by the ditch which accompanied it on its north side.

The fosse of the Wall is seen, though faintly, behind the Methodist Chapel. The private footpath leading to Carville Hall is no doubt on the site of the Wall itself. The ditch here shows itself distinctly. It often happens that when

Carville Hall

* I am indebted for this information to Mr. Reay, of Wallsend.

the Wall has been entirely removed, for the sake of its stones, the foundations are left, and used as a footpath or bridle way. Carville Hall is the Cousins' House of Horsley. As Wallsend colliery was not in existence in Horsley's day, this house was the nearest to the station of Segedunum. Hence in books we often still read that the Roman Wall begins at Cousins' House—a designation not known in the district. The fosse on the north of Carville is filled with water, and serves as a duck-pond. The stone dike which forms the fence of the next field contains many Roman stones. Stote's Houses are the Bee Houses of Horsley. On the north of them the fosse of the Wall is filled with water, and forms two ponds. Here some traces of the foundation of the Wall may be seen. About sixty yards to the south of these houses are faint traces of two tumuli, one on each side of the little valley descending to the Tyne. These may cover the ashes of some ancient British chiefs who fought and died before the Romans reached these northern parts. The cart track is now on the Wall; the fosse is less distinct—a hedge runs along it. Forty years ago the Wall in this vicinity was standing between three and four feet high, covered with brushwood. About half way between Stote's Houses and Old Walker is a small stream; at the point where the Wall crosses it several walling stones lie in its bed. West of the brook the core of the Wall is seen in the footpath. On the top of the rise, about eighty yards from the brook, is the site of the first mile-castle. It is under tillage, but its slightly elevated surface, and the number of small stones which are sprinkled over it, distinguish it from the rest of the field.

Stote's Houses.

Barrows.

Mile-castle.

The Farm-house of Old Walker is now reached. Many Roman stones appear in its walls; the fosse is used as a duck-pond. The road that is seen stretching in a straight line up the hill to Byker indicates the direction of the Wall. It is the first, but by no means the most remarkable, instance that we shall meet with of the unflinching and straightforward tendencies of this remarkable structure. The road now runs on the north of the ditch some distance. The site of the fosse all the way to Byker Hill is enclosed between hedges, and used as potato gardens. It was left waste long after the neighbouring ground was brought into tillage. Old Walker.

In the second field from Byker Hill, Mr. McLauchlan, aided by his measuring chain, lays down the position of the second mile-castle. It is seven furlongs from the last. The attentive observer will detect it by its gently swelling surface. On Byker Hill is a large quarry, which entirely obliterates the remains. Passing this and the houses near, the fosse is seen on the left of the road. A little further on, the wall on the other side of the road—enclosing the grounds of Heaton Hall—will be observed to contain many Roman stones. The Wall in this vicinity must, in the year 1725 have been standing in stately grandeur, as appears from the "Prospect of it from Byker Hill," which Stukeley gives in his *Iter Boreale*. He made this drawing because "the country being entirely undermined, it might, sometime or other, sink, and so disorder the track of this stately work." It must have remained in an encouraging state of preservation until 1800, for in the *Monthly Magazine* of that year we read, "At this period a portion of the founda- Castellum. Byker Hill.

tion of the Roman Wall was taken up at Byker Hill, for the purpose of repairing the highways."

Byker Bar. At Byker Bar the turnpike road deviates to the south; but the Wall marches right on, descending the steep bank which leads down into the Ouseburn, and then climbing the equally steep cliff on the opposite side. The Wall probably began its descent at the spot where a deserted blacksmith's shop now stands; and here once stood a mile-castle. Mile-castle. If the pilgrim can detect any traces of Wall or fosse on either of the banks of the Ouseburn valley he will be fortunate. The surface of the ground has, in some places, been removed by brick-makers, and elsewhere it is dotted over with pig-styes, potteries, flour-mills, tanneries, and knackers' yards, to such an extent as to defy all chance of success. The Wall is said to have crossed the burn a little to the south of the bridge which is a little below the railway viaduct. Red Barns. Leaving the valley, the Wall made straight for the Red Barns. In this immediate vicinity was recently to be seen a heap of loose stones (Nov. 18th, 1862), taken from an adjoining fence, which certainly had once formed a part of the Roman Wall; the hard coarse Roman mortar still adhered to them.

No traces of the Wall in its passage through the town of Newcastle are left. The necessities of a walled town, abounding in churches and monasteries, would occasion its speedy removal. Our earliest writers are not entirely agreed as to its course. It seems to have gone from the Red Barns in the direction of the Sallyport (or Carpenters' Tower); to have passed over the Wall Knoll, and afterwards to have crossed the gully of the Lort Burn, which then occupied the site of the present Dean Street. It then made in the direction of St. Nicholas' Church. Leland tells us, on the authority of Dr. Davel, then Master of St. Mary's Hospital, Newcastle, that "the church of St. Nicholas stands upon the Picts' Wall." In its passage from the town westwards, it went by St. John's Church, and in front of the palisades of the Assembly Rooms, up Westgate Hill. The range of houses called Cumberland Row very nearly represents the line of the Wall, and the present road is probably identical with the ancient military way.

II.—Pons Ælii.

Newcastle was the second station on the line. It bore the name of Pons Ælii; deriving this designation from the bridge which Hadrian, who was of the Ælian family, built over the Tyne. When the present bridge was built (1775) the previously existing structure was found to have been reared upon piers of Roman masonry. The position of the station has not been ascertained with certainty. On the north side of Collingwood Street, close to the Groat Market, strong remains of the Roman Wall were exhumed in 1810. Near the western extremity of the same street, but on its south side, another piece of Roman wall was met with in 1853. These fragments were no doubt portions of the north wall of the station. In laying down some water-pipes in Collingwood Street, in 1852, two walls of Roman masonry were exposed, which were, as near as the eye could judge, at right angles with this north wall; these must have been parts of the station. We shall probably not

The Ælian Bridge.

The station.

greatly err if we suppose Pons Ælii to have lain between St. Nicholas' Church on the one side and the Literary and Philosophical Society on the other; and, having Collingwood Street for the site of its north rampart, to have extended as far south as Baileygate, where the ground begins to dip rapidly down towards the river. When the Town Hall buildings were reared no traces of Roman building were found. This might have been expected, for the site is to the north of our supposed station. In other directions, no doubt, suburban buildings clustered round the camp. When the present County Courts (beside the Old Castle) were built, numerous Roman remains were found; and a Roman well still exists under the centre of the building.

In the museum of the Castle a few memorials of Pons

Ælii are preserved. One of them, a figure of Mercury, was found when the foundations of the Stephenson Bridge

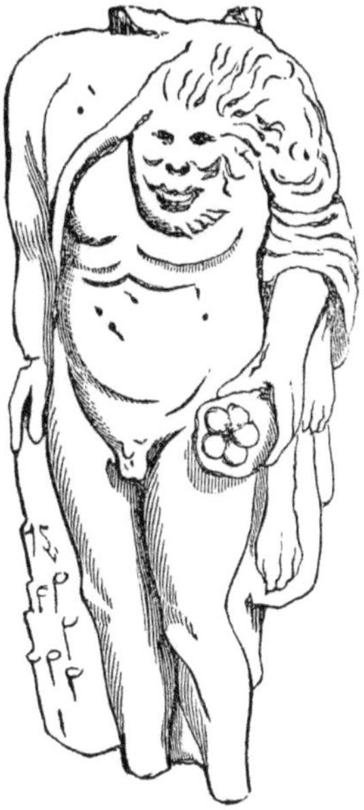

(High Level) were being dug; another, a headless figure of Hercules, was got in a garden behind the house occupied by the Poor Law Guardians; and the third, a rude altar dedicated to Silvanus, was found in pulling down the White Friar Tower (near Hanover Square). Sketches of the two former are given. A specimen of the oaken piles which, in the year 120, were driven into the bed of the river to strengthen the foundations of Hadrian's bridge, may also be seen, formed into a pilgrim's staff. Two large slabs, of wrought stone are here preserved, one of them rudely inscribed, which are supposed to have come from the Byker mile-castle; and a fine piece of embossed Samian ware, which was found when the original shaft of Wallsend pit was sunk.

According to the *Notitia*, a cohort of the Cornovii, under the command of a tribune, garrisoned Pons Ælii. Who the Cornovii were we have no means of knowing; neither does any inscription exist, either to confirm or to correct the statement of the *Notitia*.

Newcastle-upon-Tyne.

Mediæval digression.

Newcastle contains some buildings of mediæval interest, or more recent structure, on which the pilgrim may wish, in passing, to bestow some attention. The mother church of the town is dedicated to St. Nicholas. Masses of Roman ruins on the site of the present church probably led in Saxon times to the building of some homely temple, which long ago disappeared. Tradition speaks of a Norman church, founded in the reign of William Rufus. It, too, is gone, having been destroyed, it is believed, in 1216. The present church, which is mostly of a decorated character, was finished in 1350. The steeple is a subsequent addition. In 1777, the church was "beautified," and "almost all its ancient funeral monuments destroyed."—*Brand.* Rickman, says—"This church is a cross church, but has no tower at the intersection; the choir is inclosed for service; the nave is left unseated, and is of a character rather different from the eastern parts. There are some fine windows left, but some have been inserted, others altered and modernised. The steeple is the most beautiful feature of the building, and is a most excellent composition; it is early perpendicular, not much enriched, but producing a very fine effect; it is the type of which there are many imitations, but all fall far short of the original."

St. Nicholas' Church.

The inhabitants have always been proud of St. Nicholas' steeple. Lord Leven, the General of the Scotch forces that laid siege to the town in 1644, attempted to avail himself of this circumstance. Annoyed by the obstinate resistance of the inhabitants, he sent word to Sir John Marley, the Mayor, that unless the town surrendered quickly, he would fire upon the steeple. Sir John thereupon placed the chief of the Scottish prisoners on the top of the tower, and bade Lord Leven do his worst.

The Old Castle is the most complete Norman fortification remaining in England. Robert Curthose built a castle here, which must soon have perished, as we find William Rufus engaged in the work of reconstruction. Hardyng the chronicler tells us that William, in order to defray the expense of building the Castle of Newcastle and Westminster Hall, seized the revenues of nine abbeys and certain rents pertaining to the Sees of Canterbury, Winchester, and Salisbury. The present Keep was erected in the reign of Henry II. It was commenced in 1172, and finished in 1177. (See Mr. Longstaffe's paper in the *Archæologia Æliana*, N.S., vol. iv., pp. 45-139.) The Black Gate, the principal entrance into the Castle precincts, was built by Henry III. in the year 1248. When, in 1644, the Scottish forces took the town by assault, Sir John Marley and several of his associates fled to the Castle, which they held against Lord Leven for three days, when at length they were compelled to surrender. In 1812 the Corporation of Newcastle became possessed of the Castle. They put on the present roof, and raised the battlements and flag-tower. By permission of the Corporation, it is now occupied by the Society of Antiquaries of Newcastle-upon-Tyne, and the whole building is rendered easily accessible to all who are desirous of drawing from it those lessons which it is well calculated to impart.

The Castle.

The wood cut represents the castle, before the alterations of 1813, as seen from the West.

Railway Bridge.

The Stephenson Bridge (High Level) is well seen from the top of the Castle. The following memoranda respecting it may be acceptable:—The first pile was driven on October 1st, 1846. The last key, closing the arches, was driven July 10th, 1848. The length of the viaduct is 1,337 feet;

its height, from high-water mark to the line of railway, is 112 feet. The total cost of the bridge itself was £243,096; of the approaches to it, £113,057. For the land required and for compensation, there was paid £135,000; making the whole cost of the bridge and the passage of the railway through Newcastle, £491,153. But for the spirit and energy of George Hudson, the work would probably not have been attempted; it is understood to be remunerative.

III.—From Newcastle to the North Tyne.

We now pursue the Wall on its course westward. In addition to the Murus or stone Wall, we will now have the companionship of the Vallum or earth Wall. As already observed, the Vallum is not met with at either extremity of the line. With respect to the eastern end, Horsley's testimony is very emphatic. "There is not, in all the space between Cousins's House and Newcastle, the least vestige or appearance of Hadrian's Vallum, or any thing belonging to it." The Vallum is supposed to have proceeded from the southern rampart of the station of Pons Ælii, and to have run up Westgate Hill parallel with the Wall.

Westward Ho!

Vallum.

At the top of Westgate Hill, at a place called the Quarry House, Horsley found traces of a mile-castle. Neither Quarry House nor traces of a mile-castle now exist.

The first indications of the Barrier which the traveller will see are those of the Vallum. Its mounds and ditch appear the moment the last row of houses in the town—Gloucester Road—is passed. As he pursues his way to the Firth of Solway, it will seldom be out of his sight. It runs at the back of the windmill, and of the row of houses called Graingerville. It is well seen opposite the Union Work-house. On the right hand of the turnpike road the fosse of the stone Wall soon comes into sight. The additional rampart formed on its northern edge by the throwing out of the excavated materials, will here, and in many other places, be noticed.

Benwell Hill.

Benwell Hill. The third station on the line, Benwell Hill, the CONDERCVM of the Romans, is about two miles from Newcastle. Its form is nearly obliterated. It lies partly to the north of the road, and partly to the south. The northern portion is now occupied by the high-service reservoir of the Newcastle Water Company. South of the road some interesting traces of it remain. The eastern rampart and the south-east angle of the station show boldly in the grounds of G. W. Rendel, Esq.; its southern and western ramparts may be traced, though more obscurely, in the grounds of J. P. Mulcaster, Esq. The suburban buildings of this station have been extensive. One of those, on the east side, has recently been excavated by Mr. Rendel. On the sunny slope leading down to the river are manifest traces of foundations. The Vallum has come up to the southern rampart of the station; the Wall has probably joined it at the point where the road now crosses it. Altars. Two altars and other relics, the result of the recent excavations, found here are preserved on the spot. One of the altars is most tastefully adorned, and the letters on it are well cut; it is dedicated to a local god, Antenociticus, and the deities of the emperors, by Ælius Vibius, a centurion of the twentieth legion, surnamed The Valerian and Victorious. The other altar is of a ruder kind, but it has a longer inscription, which may be thus translated:—"To the god Anociticus by the decrees of our best and greatest Emperors, given under Ulpius Marcellus, a man of consular rank; Tineius Longus, of the præfecture of knights, adorned with the broad clasp, and a quæstor dedicated [this altar]." Probably the Anociticus which we have here is only a contracted form of the Antenociticus which we have on the other altar. Ulpius Marcellus was a jurist who flourished in the reigns of Antoninus Pius and Marcus Aurelius. The emperors intended are no doubt Aurelius and his colleague Lucius Verus. The altar will thus belong to a period between A.D. 161 and 169. In Mr. Mulcaster's grounds may be seen some fragments of millstones and other Roman remnants, and in particular a coping-stone, with a species of moulding, which was afterwards adopted by the Norman architects. This station was garrisoned by a troop of horse—the first wing of the Asturians, a people of Spain. The Romans are supposed to have wrought the coal in the vicinity of Benwell. When the lower water-reservoir was formed here, three or four years ago, some ancient coal workings were exposed, but nothing was found to indicate decisively the period to which they belonged. They may have been Roman.

Ancient Coal Pits.

Leaving Condercum, we again pursue our journey westward. The road runs for several miles upon the foundation of the Wall. Formerly the facing stones were in many places seen protruding through the "metal;" but since the diversion of the greater part of the traffic from the road to the railway, the remnants of this great relic of antiquity have, in several instances, been removed to supply material for mending the turnpike. The north fosse, as we pursue

our journey, becomes more distinct on the right hand. De-
East Denton scending Benwell Hill, the village of East Denton is reached. Here, on the left hand side, we meet, for the first time, with a remnant of the Wall rising above the ground. The cut

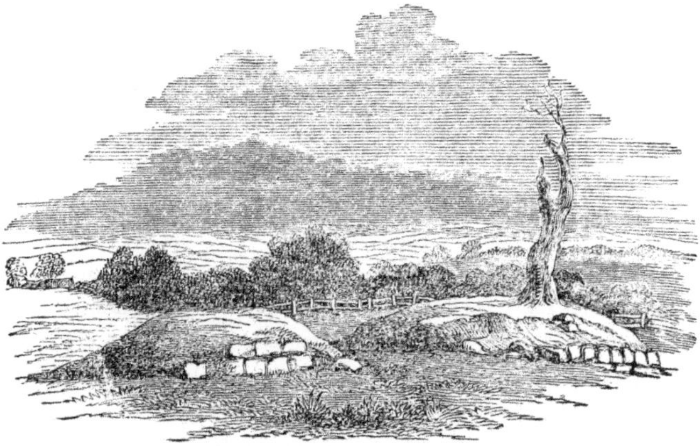

shews it. It is 9½ feet wide. The trunk of the apple tree which long grew upon it fell two winters ago. Denton Hall, on the right, is soon reached. Here a few sculptured stones from the Wall are preserved. Opposite to Denton Hall the core of the Wall is in good preservation, and at the bottom of the field on the south all the features of the

III Miles. Vallum may be noticed. The next village is West Denton.

West Denton. Here, before coming to the brook, the traces of a mile-castle may be observed amongst a mass of ruins. Let the pilgrim now advance a few yards, and examine the southern extremity of the culvert which carries the road over the brook. Here he will see, beneath the modern structure, the Roman drain which conveyed the water under the Wall. Each side of the channel is formed of a series of

Roman Culvert.

massive stones, set on edge; others, lying flat, form the covering. The passage is about two feet wide, and the same in height. This seems to have been the usual mode of crossing brooks. Stukeley, speaking of an instance in the vicinity of Carvoran, says, "I remarked that where the Wall passes over a little rivulet the foundation is laid with broad flat stones, square, having intervals between sufficiently large for the passage of water." A wide spanning arch would, in dry seasons, have invited an influx of hostile Caledonians. The geologist will be interested in knowing that, a little to the south of this spot, very near where the ditch of the Vallum crosses the brook, the course of the Ninety-fathom Dyke is still to be seen. This "fault will be detected by the perpendicularity of the strata." (McL., p. 15). At West Denton the Murus and Vallum are about 200 yards apart; after this they slowly converge until they

Ninety-Fathom Dyke.

reach Walbottle Dean, where they are but sixty yards distant from each other. After that they keep nearly parallel, and in close contiguity until reaching Rutchester. Ascending the hill from West Denton, the fosse of the Wall is boldly developed. The Vallum is feeble. Passing the fourth mile-stone, we arrive at Chapel House. The view here is extensive. On the south of the road Horsley observed "some foundations of stone ramparts." They are now completely eradicated. A little beyond this—half way down the field—we meet with the site of another *castellum;* it is barely discernible. On the slope of this hill and the rise of the next, several traces of the Wall are to be seen in the road. Passing Walbottle (*botle* is the Saxon for an abode), we come to the fifth mile-stone; the Vallum here is good, and it is well seen rising the hill before us. Opposite the farm-house called Walbottle Dean House, another castellum has stood; it can only be detected by the elevation of its site. There is a beautiful prospect from it. No traces of the bridge by which the Wall crossed the dean remain. Proceeding onwards, a lane crosses the road. Turning up the lane for a few yards, we get a sight of a tumulus, called Deafley or Dewley Hill—about half a mile distant—the burial place, probably, of some ancient British chief. The turning to the left hand takes us to Newburn. At Newburn the river, for the first time, becomes fordable. In ancient times it was consequently a place of importance. Its knolls bear marks of early fortifications, and several stones in the present church are undoubtedly Roman. There is reason to believe that the Romans laid a framework of stone across the bed of the river to improve the ford. In

Chapel House.

Walbottle.

Newburn.

1346 David King of Scotland crossed the ford in his way to Neville's Cross. In 1640 the Scotch forces under General Lesley defeated the troops of Charles I. at Newburn.

After passing the sixth mile-stone, Throckley Bank Top is reached. Both the fosse of the Wall and the Vallum show boldly. Another mile-castle is reached; besides the gentle elevation, the difference in the colour of its soil or the tint of its vegetation will often be noticed. The traveller will observe that very often the gate into the field is placed on the spot where a mile-castle stood. The reason is obvious; the ruins of the building formed a hard surface, which was useless for agricultural purposes, but most excellent for sustaining traffic. A little further on, a range of houses attracts the eye on the right of the road. It is the Frenchmen's Row, originally built for the workmen employed in Heddon Colliery, but afterwards used as the residence of a number of refugees, who fled to England on the occasion of the first French Revolution. The dial was constructed by them.

VI Miles.

Frenchmen's Row.

On the top of a little eminence, at which we arrive before reaching Heddon-on-the-Wall, the north fosse is deeper than we have yet seen it. The works of the Vallum, about fifty yards to the south, are also finely developed. In both cases the ditch is cut through the freestone rock. In the sides of the south ditch the tool-marks of the excavators are visible. Before entering the village, let the traveller clamber over the tree-crowned wall which skirts the road on his left. He will here see an interesting fragment of the Wall. Its north face is destroyed, but four courses of its southern face remain in excellent preservation. At Heddon-on-the-Wall,

Heddon-on-the-Wall.

the Wall is only about thirty-five yards from the ditch of the Vallum. The fosse of the Vallum is seen cutting boldly through the village; in the low ground it is used as a pond. A castellum must have stood hereabouts; it has probably been destroyed by the erection of this village. The seventh mile-stone is passed just as we leave the place. The road that turns off to the left leads to Horsley and Corbridge.

The Military Road.

The road that we have been travelling upon, and which we are to keep for several miles further, goes nearly straight forward. It is General Wade's Military Road. When the Pretender's forces appeared before Carlisle in 1745, the royal troops were lying at Newcastle, where the enemy had been expected. At that time no road that would bear the transit of artillery existed between Newcastle and Carlisle, so that General Wade was obliged to leave Carlisle to the mercy of the enemy, and proceed in search of him by a southerly route. He met him at Preston; with what effect is well known. After this the road between Newcastle and Carlisle, now known throughout the district as "The Military Road," was made.

John Wesley on mural matters.

This digression prepares us for a brief memorandum from the pen of that eminent man, John Wesley. He writes—"Wednesday, 21 May, 1755. I preached at Nafferton, near Horsley, about thirteen miles from Newcastle. We rode chiefly on the new western road, which lies on the old Roman Wall. Some part of this is still to be seen, as are the remains of most of the towers, which were built a mile distant from each other, quite from sea to sea. But where are the men of renown who built them, and who once made all the land tremble? Crumbled into dust! Gone hence, to be no more seen, till the earth shall give up her dead!"

Not much that calls for observation occurs before reaching the next station—Rutchester. About midway between Heddon-on-the-Wall and Rutchester is the site of a mile-castle; it is very indistinct. VIII Miles.

Rutchester.

Rutchester, the ancient VINDOBALA, is the fourth station on the line of the Wall. It was garrisoned by the first cohort of Frixagi, or as it should probably be written, Frisii. The Frisians were one of the great tribes of North-western Germany. Unless the traveller be on his guard, he may pass through the middle of Vindobala without knowing it. A lane crosses the road just as you come up to it.

The Station. The great Wall seems to have joined the station at its gateways, leaving a considerable portion of the camp projecting to the north, and a still larger to the south of it. The station, the general form of which may be discerned, has had an area of about 3½ acres. The turnpike road probably represents its *via principalis.* To the north of the road the station is under the plough, but the general elevation of its surface, and the slight, though yearly diminishing traces of its ditch, serve sufficiently well to mark its position. South of the road, also, the western and southern ramparts remain in a fair state of preservation. The farm-buildings are all to the south of the camp.

The Vallum here, as is usually the case in the immediate vicinity of stations, is indistinct; but it seems to have joined the fort in a line with its southern rampart. The suburbs have been to the south of the station. The present farm-house, which has recently been fitted up for the occasional residence of the proprietor of the estate, Thomas James, Esq., of Otterburn Castle, is formed on the nucleus of a mediæval stronghold; some of its ancient features are retained. To the west of the farm-house, on the brow of the hill, a trough-like excavation has been made in the solid rock. Its use is not known. It was once popularly called

The Giant's Grave.

the Giant's Grave. Another account of its use is recorded in Sir David Smith's MSS., now preserved in Alnwick Castle: "The old peasants here have a tradition that the Romans made a beverage somewhat like beer of the bells of heather (heath), and that this trough was used in the process of making such drink."—The opinion long prevailed in Northumberland, that the *Picts* had the art of preparing an intoxicating liquor from heather-bells, and that the secret died with them.—The cistern is 12 feet long, 4½ broad, and 2 deep, and has a hole close to the bottom at one end. When discovered, in 1766, it had a partition of masonry across it, and contained many decayed bones, and an iron implement described as being like a three-footed

Altars.

candlestick. In 1844 four altars were discovered a few yards to the west of the Giant's Grave. One of them is shown in the wood-cut. The sculpture on its base, as well as other circumstances, leaves no doubt that the god intended is not the one true and living God, but Mithras, the Eastern Apollo. The altar is neatly designed; a wreath encircles the word DEO, and two palm branches

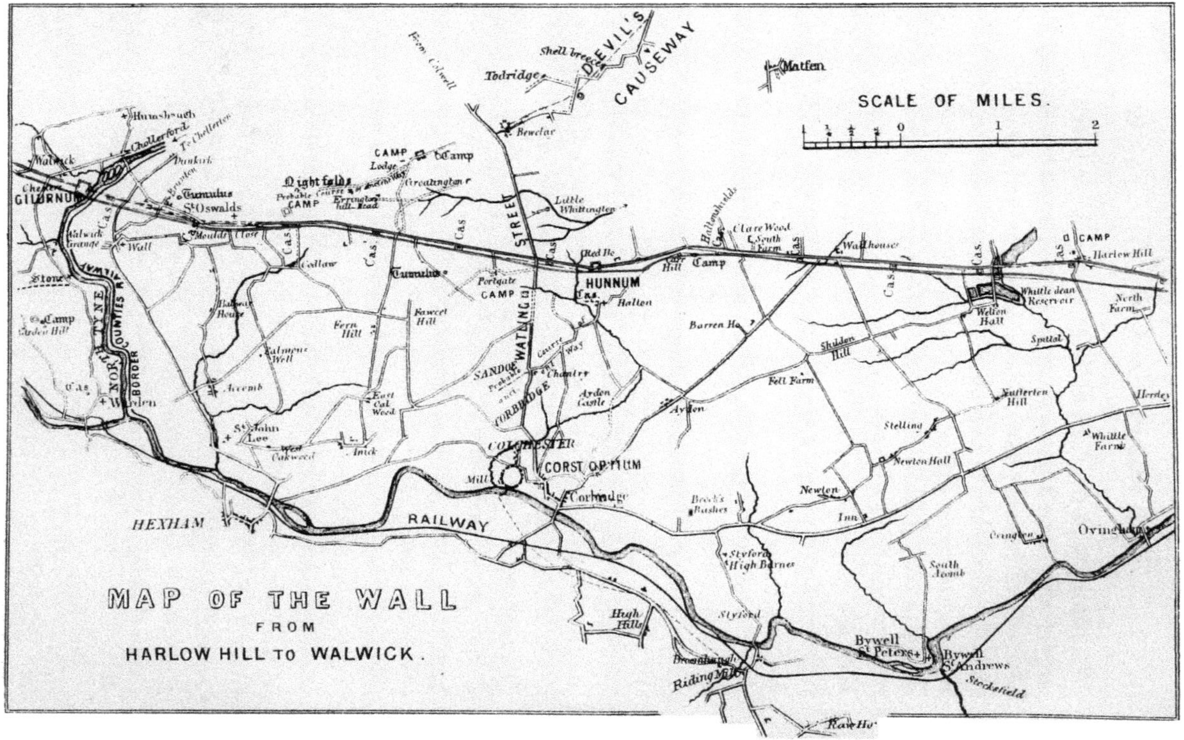
MAP OF THE WALL
FROM
HARLOW HILL TO WALWICK.
SCALE OF MILES.
0
1
2
DEVIL'S CAUSEWAY
Matfen
Todridge
Bewclay
From Colwell
CAMP
Camp
Lodge
Nightfolds
Probable Course
CAMP
Errington hill Head
Greatington
Tumulus
St Oswalds
Little Whittington
STREET
WATLING
Cas.
Humshaugh
Chollerford
To Chollerton
Walwick
Chesters
CILURNUM
Walwick Grange
Wall
Collaw
Tumulus
Portgate
CAMP
HUNNUM
Red Ho
Halton
Carr Hill
Camp
Halton Shields
Clare Wood
South Farm
Walltouse
Harlow Hill
Whittle dean Reservoir
Welton Hall
North Farm
Spittal
Shildon Hill
Barren Ho
Fell Farm
Stone
Camp
Warden Hill
NORTH TYNE
COUNTIES RAILWAY
BORDER
Warden
Acomb
Fern Hill
Fawcet Hill
East Cal Wood
Anick
St John Lee
West Oakwood
SANDOE
Chantry
CORBRIDGE
Probable Course
Way
Aydon Castle
Aydon
COLCHESTER
CORSTOPITUM
Mill
Corbridge
HEXHAM
RAILWAY
Brock's Bushes
Styford High Barnes
High Hill
Styford
Broomhaugh
Riding Mill
Newton
Inn
Newton Hall
Stelling
Nafferton Hill
Whittle Farm
Heddon
Ovington
Ovingham
South Acomb
Bywell St Peters
Bywell St Andrews
Stocksfield
Raw Ho

wave over it. The inscription may thus be read in English—"Lucius Sentius Castus [a centurion], of the sixth legion, piously dedicated this altar to the god [Mithras]." It is now at Otterburn. Most of the stones of the farm-buildings and adjacent fences are Roman. A few fragments of inscriptions are built up in the walls; one, in a coach-house, bears the letters, AVR. RIN. XIT. NIS. It is no doubt part of a monumental tablet; when complete it would probably be—*Diis Manibus Aurelius Victorinus vixit annis. . . . .*

We now continue our journey. About one-third of a mile forward, on a knoll, the site of another mile-castle occurs. Presently we pass on the left of the road a house formerly known as "The Iron-sign;" but which has ceased to be a place of public entertainment. Some of the buildings are entirely composed of Roman stones. In the wall of a stable abutting upon the road, are some centurial and sculptured stones. They are read with difficulty, but in a favourable light one of them seems to be COH. VIII.; another, ɔHOS. LVPI.; and a third, COH. VIII. BRIT. A side light is the best for reading weathered inscriptions. Passing the ninth mile-stone, we stand upon the top of an eminence, Centurial Stones.

called Round Hill, or sometimes Eppie's Hill. We have here a good view of Harlow Hill and the adjacent country. The north fosse is very distinct, forming a deep groove on the right of the road all the way to Harlow Hill. The Wall and the Vallum are at this point within thirty yards of each other. They soon separate; for whilst the Wall inclines to the north in order to secure, in conformity with its usual practice, the high ground, the Vallum continues to move onward in a nearly straight line. In doing so it runs along the flanks of Harlow Hill. Had the Vallum been an independent barrier, it would probably have kept to the high ground. From a point opposite to the next mile-castle, to Carr Hill, a distance of five miles, the Vallum goes in a perfectly straight line.

A little more than half a mile beyond Round Hill, we pass the site of a mile-castle; the Vallum is here 400 yards from the Wall. In passing over the summit of Harlow Hill, the foundations of the Wall may be seen in the fold yards on the south side of the village. A mile-castle has stood here, but no traces of it now exist. On the high ground north of the village are the remains of a tumulus and entrenchments. The Romans would not leave so important a position undefended. From the quarries under this summit the builders of the Wall seem to have obtained both freestone and lime. Some barrows to the north of this place, and graves filled with human bones, confirm the traditionary account of bloody battles having been fought here in "the troublesome times."

Harlow Hill.

Digression relating to the Water Company.

Descending the hill, we come to the reservoirs of the Whittle Dean Water Company, by which Newcastle is supplied. These are eight in number, and on the day that the author last passed that way (March 21st, 1863), contained 530 million gallons of water. Newcastle requires a daily supply of 4½ millions of gallons. When the Company was first formed, it was thought sufficient to impound the water brought down by the two chief feeders of the Whittle Dean. This being found inadequate, additional stores were sought from the river Pont. The demand still rising, an aqueduct has been extended for several miles in a north-west direction, bringing into the reservoirs the waters of the Hallington Burns, the Small Burn, and other streams. Further measures are contemplated, in order to secure an adequate supply in times of extreme drought. The water is conveyed from the reservoirs to Newcastle by means of iron pipes sunk in the ground. The town has in several instances been put to serious inconvenience by the bursting of the pipes. A plan is now being carried out for securing a second series of pipes between the reservoirs and town, by which this evil will be remedied, and the water carried down in a sufficient quantity.

Advantage of Roman Aqueducts.

There cannot be a doubt that the Company would have consulted their pecuniary interests as well as their credit if they had acted, in the first instance, upon the Roman principle, bringing their supplies to the outskirts of the town by means of an aqueduct, having in the course of it, at distances of not more than a mile, small reservoirs for filtering the water, and keeping up a continuity of supply when local repairs required a temporary stoppage at the source. It is said that the chairman of the Company, the present Sir William Armstrong, at the very commencement of operations, urged as strongly as possible the adoption of an aqueduct, but his wise counsel was unwisely over-ruled.

The village of Welton is about half a mile to the south of the road. Its most prominent feature is the ancient

WeltonHall

fortlet called Welton Hall. It is built entirely of Roman stones. Over the door are the initials and date—WW. 1614. Strange stories are still told of the enormous strength of Old Will of Welton. Ascending the hill, just after passing the reservoirs, the site of another mile-castle is seen on the left hand. At this point the Vallum, after crossing one of the reservoirs, again comes into close companionship with the Wall. At the usual distance ($7\frac{1}{2}$ furlongs) westward of the castle just named, the site of another may be discerned. It is about a furlong west of the Robin Hood Inn, where a

Low Wall Houses.

road turns down to a farm-house. Wall Houses are next reached. Between this point and the fourteenth mile-stone all the lines of the Barrier are developed in a degree that is quite inspiriting. The north fosse is, for some distance, planted with trees, which will, for a considerable time, save it from the plough. Another little village, called High Wall Houses is next approached. After passing the turnpike-gate, a road on the left leads to Corbridge, distant about four miles, and Hexham about seven miles. About a

Shildon Hill.

mile to the south of us is Shildon Hill, which forms a conspicuous feature in the landscape. It has an oval-shaped entrenchment on its summit, belonging, probably, to the ancient British era. At Matfen-Piers Lodge there is another mile-castle. The Wall, as seen in the road, is a little less than eight feet thick. The road on the right leads to

XIV Miles.

Matfen. At Matfen Hall, the seat of Sir Edward Blackett, Bart., are several important inscribed and sculptured stones, and other antiquities derived from the Wall, especially from the station of Hunnum.

At Halton Shields was another *castellum*, though all decided traces of it are now obliterated.—"Like the man at Halton Shields," was a saying that was common a while ago. This celebrated personage set off on a journey, and after travelling laboriously all night found himself at his own back door next morning.—On the top of the next summit, Carr Hill, the facing stones of the Wall are seen in the road, and the angle which it here makes, bending away to the south, may be observed. It measures 9 feet 6 inches in width. The Wall and Vallum are here fifty-five yards apart. They go on in tolerable parallelism for some distance, when the Vallum suddenly bends to the south, evidently to avoid a small barrow-like elevation called Down Hill. Having done this, it returns as suddenly to something like its former direction. The Wall pursues a straightforward course, and cuts across the hill. These appearances strongly corroborate the opinion, that the various lines of the fortification are but parts of one great scheme. If the Vallum had been constructed as an independent defence against a northern foe, and nearly a century before the Wall, an elevation, which so entirely commands the Vallum, would surely not have been left open to the enemy; especially as it would be just as easy to take the Vallum along the north flank of the hill as the south. Passing Halton Red House, we reach the station of HUNNUM.

Halton Shields.

Carr Hill.

Down Hill.

Halton Chesters.

The Station of Hunnum.

The Wall came up to the lateral gateways of this camp; consequently the turnpike-road, its present representative, goes through the midst of it. Unless the traveller be on the alert, he will pass through the station without knowing it, as did Sandy Gordon the Scottish Antiquary, and as did William Hutton the first time they visited it. The Vallum came up to the southern rampart. Horsley gave this camp the name of Halton Chesters, from the village of Halton, which lies about half a mile to the south of it. This station has the usual rectangular form, but it possesses this peculiarity, that an angular portion has, as it were, been cut out of its north-west corner. The nature of the ground has probably dictated this arrangement. The station has contained an area of four acres and a quarter. The distance between the last station, Rutchester, and this is greater than usual, being seven miles and two furlongs in a direct line. The station of Hunnum was garrisoned by a troop of horse, called in the *Notitia*, "Ala Saviniana" or "Sabiniana." This troop probably took its name from Sabina, the wife of Hadrian. There is reason to believe that the Empress accompanied Hadrian to Britain, and that the imperial court was established here for the winter of 119-120 (*Merivale*, v. vii., p. 438.) The only inscription confirming the *Notitia* in its statement of the occupation of Hunnum, is one which was first noticed by Camden, and is now preserved at Cambridge. It is part of a monumental slab, dedicated to the shades of Noricus, who died at the age of 30, by Messorius Magnus, a brother of the deceased, and a *duplaris* of the *Ala Sabiniana*.

Sabina in Britain.

The portion of the station north of the road was brought into cultivation in the year 1827. It is called the "Brunt-ha'penny Field," from the number of corroded copper coins which were picked up in it. Numerous buildings, most carefully constructed, were found in it. One of them was an elaborate structure, containing at least eleven apartments. These were heated by the transmission of hot air under their floors and up their sides. The idea has been extensively adopted that all the buildings provided with hypocausts were public baths. The Romans were great bathers, but we must not overlook the difference between the climate of Italy and Britain. Warmth would be the first requisite here. Nearly all the remains found in Northumberland prove that the necessities of war were chiefly attended to, not the requirements of luxury. The remains of "The Baths" at Hunnum were most carefully examined and described by the Rev. John Hodgson and Mr. Dobson (*Hist. Nor.*, Pt. II., vol. iii., p. 317); but though we are told which was the *apodyterium*, which the *tepidarium*, the *caldarium*, and the *frigidarium*, nothing is said about those essential requisites in a public bathing establishment—the pipes for the introduction of the water, the boilers for heating, and the basins for holding it. A portion of one of the smallest of the chambers here was indeed walled off and carefully lined with cement, so as to form a reservoir, ten feet long by seven feet three inches broad, but this was the only real indication of a bath. Similar cisterns have been found at Cilurnum, Borcovicus, and elsewhere; these were probably the only arrangements made for bathing, even in the dwellings of the tribunes and the prefects, and these

Extensive Bathing Establishments questioned.

were probably supplied by hand, with hot or cold water, at the command of the master of the house. The whole of this building was removed as soon as it was discovered. The part of the station which is to the south of the road has a gentle slope and a fair exposure to the sun. It is known by the name of the Chesters; in Horsley's day it had the additional designation of Silverhill, no doubt from the discovery, on some occasion, of a number of denarii in it. As it has not been recently ploughed, it exhibits, with considerable distinctness, the lines of the outer entrenchments, as well as the contour of the ruined buildings and streets of the interior. The road to Halton runs through the middle of the station, probably on the very site of the old Roman *via* leading from the Prætorian to the Decuman gate. The suburbs have covered a fine tract of pasture ground to the south.

Halton Castle and Church.

Halton Castle and Church are chiefly composed of Roman stones. In the church-yard is a Roman altar placed upside down, but its inscription is obliterated. In the farm-buildings attached to the castle are some Roman mouldings and a weathered figure, probably part of a sepulchral slab.

On leaving the station, it will be noticed how much the defile on its west side strengthens the military position of the camp. About a furlong before reaching Portgate the faint traces of a mile-castle may be seen.

Passing the sixteenth mile-stone, we come to another *castellum*, and continuing to ascend the hill, we soon reach

The Watling Street.

the ancient Watling Street, which crosses the Wall at right angles. This road, which was probably formed by Agricola, in his first advance into Scotland, is in many places, as here, still used as a highway; in others it is grass-grown and deserted, but even in these instances it retains, often for miles together, all the features of its original construction. The Watling Street leaves the Scottish border at Chew Green, where are several camps of remarkable construction. It passes the stations of BREMENIUM, High Rochester, and HABITANCUM, Risingham, and after crossing the Wall, proceeds southward to CORSTOPITUM, Corchester, and so to the stations at Ebchester and Lanchester, in the county of Durham.

There can be little doubt that the station of HUNNUM was intended to guard the passage of the Wall by the Street.

The Wall and Vallum are parallel in this place, and are about eighty yards apart. The earthworks now become exceedingly interesting, and continue to be so for the next two or three miles. The north fosse is in many places very bold; the materials that have been turned out of it are lying on the outer margin, rough and untrimmed, as if the labourers had left the work but to obtain some refreshment, and were about to return to it. Ascending the hill, on the top of which is a fir plantation, the Wall may in one place be measured six feet wide; a little further forward it has increased to nine feet six inches in width. Before reaching the plantation, a mile-castle will be observed. At this point it will be well for the pilgrim to forsake the turnpike-road, and examine the Vallum. He will not find it in a more perfect state in any other part of the line. Old Mr. Hutton was charmed with it. "I climbed over a stone wall," he says, "to examine the wonder; measured the whole in every direction; surveyed it with surprise, with delight; was fascinated, and unable to proceed; forgot I

The Earthworks good.

Mr. Hutton's enthusiasm.

was upon a wild common, a stranger, and the evening approaching; lost in astonishment, I was not able to move."

On passing the crown of the hill, and beginning the descent, the Wall may be measured (in the road) ten feet five inches in width.

Errington Hill-Head.

XVIII Miles.

Before reaching the eighteenth mile-stone, the site of another mile-castle may be distinctly noticed. On Errington Hill-Head, about half a mile to the north of this point, are some ancient encampments; they command a magnificent view of the Erring-Burn and of the valley of North Tyne. About a furlong before reaching the nineteenth mile-stone, the feeble traces of a mile-castle may perhaps be recognised. Directly opposite to this, on the north of the Wall, and about a furlong from it, "is a small quadrangular enclosure, on the top of the crag, which is presumed to be the remains of a small Roman camp, made to protect the workmen while they were quarrying and building the Wall." (*McL.*, p. 24.) This camp has been a good deal disturbed.

Temporary Camps.

In several other instances, which we shall notice as they occur, Mr. McLauchlan, found a similar arrangement to exist—a small earthen camp opposite a mile-castle. There can be no doubt, that the reason he assigns for them, is the true one. This camp is to the north of the Wall; in nearly every other instance the camp is to the south of the Wall. Advancing a little further along the road, we observe north of the Wall a round hill, which to all appearance is a tumulus. In front of one of the houses at St. Oswald's-Hill-Head, a centurial stone is built up bearing the inscription COH. VIII. || ↃCECILI || CLIME.—The century or company of Cecilius Clemens (?) of the eighth cohort. Immediately south of this place, distant about a quarter of a mile, is Fallowfield Fell, where the Roman quarryman, Carantinus, has left his name upon the rock, as already stated (p. 32). The "written rock," is not easily found in consequence of its being but slightly elevated above the general level. The view from the Fell is very extensive and fine.

Onwards, we come to St. Oswald's Church. Opposite to it is a field called Mould's Close, where, according to local tradition, the hottest of the fight between King Oswald and Cadwalla raged. Bede's account of the battle is as follows: —" This last king (Oswald), after the death of his brother Eanfrid, advanced with an army, small indeed in number, but strengthened with the faith of Christ; and the impious commander of the Britons was slain, though, he had most numerous forces, which he boasted nothing could withstand, at a place in the English tongue called Denisesburn, that is, Denis's-brook. This place is shown to this day, and held in much veneration, where Oswald being about to engage, erected the sign of the holy cross, and on his knees prayed to God that he would assist his worshippers in their great distress. It is further reported, that the cross being made in haste, and the hole dug in which it was to be fixed, the King himself, full of faith, laid hold of it, and held it with both his hands till it was set fast by throwing in the earth; and this done, raising his voice, he cried to his army, 'Let us all kneel, and jointly beseech the true and living God Almighty, in his mercy, to defend us from the haughty and fierce enemy; for He knows that we have undertaken a just war for the safety of our nation.' All did as he had commanded, and accordingly advancing

St. Oswald's Church.

The Battle A.D. 635.

towards the enemy with the first dawn of the day, they obtained the victory, as their faith deserved. In that place of prayer very many miraculous cures are known to have been performed, as a token and memorial of the King's faith; for even to this day, many are wont to cut off small chips of the wood of the holy cross, which being put into water, men or cattle drinking of, or sprinkled with that water, are immediately restored to health. The place in the English tongue is called Hefenfeld, or the Heavenly Field. . . The same place is near the Wall with which the Romans formerly enclosed the island from sea to sea, to restrain the fury of the barbarous nations, as has been said before. Hither, also, the brothers of the church of Hagulstad, which is not far from thence, repair yearly on the day before that on which King Oswald was afterwards slain, to watch there for the health of his soul, and having sung many psalms, to offer for him in the morning the sacrifice of the holy oblation. And since that good custom has spread, they have lately built and consecrated a church there, which has attached additional sanctity and honour to that place." (*Bede's Ecclesiastical History*, b. III. ch. vii., Giles's translation.)

Denisesburn Burn, probly near Dilston.

The Rev. Wm. Greenwell has adduced strong evidence to show that Denisesburn was in the vicinity of Dilston. The existence of the church fixes the spot where the cross was raised, and where probably, also, the battle was begun, but the fight may have extended towards Dilston, and the slaughter of Cadwalla taken place there.

Plane-trees FarmHouse.

Some faint traces of the next mile-castle may be seen at the field-gate on the right of the road, opposite Plane-trees

Farm House. The house is in the ditch of the Vallum. A little further on, also on the right of the road, is the Black-Pasture Quarry, which yields stone of the same nature as that used in the Wall in this vicinity. The pedestal of the monument to George Stephenson, in Newcastle, is made of stone from this quarry. When last visited by the writer, some squared blocks, containing seventy cubic feet of stone, were lying ready for transport. The extreme durability of the stone is proved by the fact that the facing-stones of the Wall here have stood the accidents of more than seventeen centuries without the least indication of decay. In selecting a stone for the building of the Houses of Parliament, a pilgrim by the line of Hadrian's Wall might have been consulted with advantage. Before reaching the twentieth mile-stone, we come to Plane-trees Field, where, on the left of the road, a conspicuous piece of the Wall remains. It has, in some places, five courses of facing-stones entire; the grout of the interior, which rises still higher, gives root to some fine old thorns. The stones in the Wall here are of a larger size than usual, probably owing to the near vicinity of the quarry. In the grounds of Brunton—the residence of Major Waddilove—a little below this, a small piece of the Wall is to be seen, in a state of very great perfection. It is seven feet high, and presents nine courses of facing-stones entire. The mortar of the five lower courses is good; the face of the south side is gone. The ditch, along which we walk in coming to this relic, is very boldly developed; and being, during the summer months, thickly covered with ferns and wild flowers, is an object of great interest.

Roman Quarry.

Brunton.

The road, which for nearly the whole distance from

Deviation of the Road.

Newcastle has run upon the line of the Wall, now deviates considerably to the north of it. This was done by the Government Surveyor, in order to take advantage of a bridge which crossed the river at Chollerford. This was no doubt the bridge, for the repairs of which thirteen days' relaxation of enjoined penance was granted to contributors by Bishop Skirlaw, in the time of Richard II. Unfortunately it was carried away by the great flood of 1771, when the present bridge was built.

Ancient Bridge.

On the east bank of the river towards the north is a conspicuous building, called Cocklaw Tower. It is roofless, but forms a fine and characteristic specimen of the border fortress. On the walls of one of its apartments are traces of fresco-painting. On the opposite side of the river, though not seen but on a nearer approach, is Haughton Castle, the seat of George Crawshay, Jun., Esq. The situation of this castle is most lovely, and the building itself, consisting as it does of an ecclesiastical fabric, adapted to the purposes of border warfare, furnishes a study of considerable intricacy, but great interest.

Cocklaw Tower.

The George at Chollerford.

The inn at Chollerford is, as is well known to many anglers, and some antiquaries, an exceedingly comfortable one.

We now return to the Wall at Brunton. It continues its onward course to the North Tyne in a straight line. A little before reaching the railway a gently elevated mound indicates the site of a mile-castle. Next we meet with the most remarkable feature on the whole line of the Wall—the bridge over the North Tyne. This is nearly half a mile down the river from the railway station. As foot passengers are usually debarred from walking on the

The Roman Bridge over the North Tyne.

line, a traveller approaching it from this quarter should take the stile at the east end of Chollerford Bridge, and find his way through fields and along the river's brink to the object of his search.

The lines both of Wall and Vallum may be distinguished as they approach the river. The Wall, as it enters the little plantation on the river's brink, has been laid bare. It is six feet four inches thick, and in one place stands eight feet eight inches high. It terminates in a square building or *castellum*, formed of stones of the same character as those used in the Wall. Several lairs of wood ashes were found when this building was excavated. In front of it we have the land abutment of the bridge. It consists of a solid mass of masonry, of a form well calculated to resist the thrust of the descending stream, and the regurgitation of the waters when passed. The abutment presents to the river a face of twenty-two feet, and from it the platform of the bridge would spring. From each side of this projecting face the walls retire in an oblique direction. The southern portion of the abutment has originally been formed upon the same plan as the northern, but an addition has afterwards been made to it, probably to give increased space for defensive works. In the northern part of the abutment, five courses of facing-stones remain, giving a height above the foundation course of six feet. Some of the stones are very large; one is four feet ten inches long, and eighteen inches in height. The stone is from the Black Pasture Quarry, already referred to (p. 73). All the facing-stones have been placed in their position by the luis, and they have been bound together by rods of iron imbedded

Land Abutment of the Bridge.

Iron Cramps.

in lead The grooves for the rods, and, in some places, the lead remain. The peculiar feathered tooling of the facing-stones will be noticed. It is the opinion of some antiquaries that, whilst the great mass of the bridge is the work of Hadrian, these facing-stones are the work of Severus. It is probable that, by his time, the bridge would require repairs, and these he would be able to effect, both here and in other parts of the mural fortress, before entering upon his Caledonian expedition. At Housesteads and many other places stones that have evidently been used in repairs have this peculiar kind of broaching. One other circumstance requires attention. Imbedded in the centre of the abutment is a piece of masonry which is independent of all the rest, and has the form of a water pier. The river in this part of its course has a tendency to recede from its eastern bank and encroach upon its western. The present abutment is some distance from the river, while that upon the other side is entirely submerged. There can be little doubt that this tendency has always existed, and that the pier which we now see in the middle of the land-abutment of Hadrian's Bridge was formerly one of the water piers of a bridge of earlier date, probably erected by Agricola, for the purpose of communication with the fortress of Cilurnum on the opposite bank of the river. The stones of this pier are bound together, individually, by wedge-shaped cramps, not grouped by long rods, as the facing stones of the abutment are.

Stones with Feathered Tooling.

One of Agricola's Water Piers.

A Timber Platform

The platform of this bridge was undoubtedly of timber. Several of the stones which lie on the ground have grooves in them for admitting the spars. No arch stones have been found among the ruins.

From coins, from the sculptures on Trajan's column, and other authentic sources of information, we learn that the approaches to a bridge on an enemy's frontier were always defended by appropriate fortifications. Here, particularly on the south side, as already observed, there was ample space for these defensive bulwarks. When the whole structure was complete it must have had a very formidable appearance. Towers.

A covered way, evidently posterior to any of the other works, will be observed crossing the abutment and cutting through the Wall. It goes beyond the extent of the excavations in both directions. It is formed in a great measure of stones that have been used in the bridge. As it is founded upon a bed of silt at least a yard thick, its construction cannot have taken place until the works of the bridge had been overwhelmed by some terrible devastation. No probable conjecture has yet been formed of its use. The idea of a water-course naturally rises in the mind; but the joints of the passage are by no means close, and, though covered on the top, the bottom of it consists simply of the sandy alluvium of the river. Most of the slabs which form the covering have been snapped across, apparently by the weight of the deposit upon them, though some of them are two feet thick; they were found precisely as they now lie. A more recent Covered Way.

Several stones among the debris will attract attention. Amongst them is one about four feet in length, resembling an axletree. It has orifices as if for receiving handspikes. Its use is not known, but it has been suggested that it may have been used in pounding the mortar, or it may have been part of the machinery of a ballista. There is also a circular Peculiar Stones.

shaft, about 9 feet long and 2 feet in diameter, which has several peculiarities. Unhappily no inscribed stone has been found to detail the history of the bridge. One large slab was found; but the greater portion of it having been exposed to the roll of the river for centuries, its inscription is entirely obliterated, except the last three lines, which happened to be protected, but which tell us nothing. They are

Obliterated Inscription.

. . . .

RANTE AELIO

LONGINO

PRAEF EQQ.

The works were no doubt executed under the inspection of (*curante*) or by the order of (*imperante*) Ælius Longinus, a prefect of cavalry; but as we have not previously met with a prefect of this name, we are in ignorance of the date of the inscription.

Two years ago the whole of this piece of masonry was buried under the accumulated deposits of the river, and the more effectually to conceal the architectural treasure beneath, a thriving plantation occupied the surface. Mr. William Coulson of Corbridge, who had acquired considerable experience as an explorator of Roman remains at Bremenium, suspected the truth. It was at his suggestion, and partly under his superintendence, that the recent excavations were undertaken by Mr. Clayton, the proprietor of the stations of CILURNUM, BORCOVICUS, and VINDOLANA, and of extensive tracts of Wall between and beyond them—a gentleman to whom, more than any other, the antiquary is indebted for the preservation and skilful display of the best remnants of imperial power in Britain.

The reader is referred to the frontispiece for a plan of the abutment. In a paper by Mr. Clayton, in the *Archæologia Æliana*, N.S., vol. vi., p. 80, he will find a fuller account, than the limits of this little volume allow, of this important structure.

We now turn to the other works of the bridge. There have been three water piers. It has been ascertained, by partial excavation, that one of them lies immediately under the eastern bank of the river. Two others are, when the water is low and placid, to be seen in the bed of the stream. Blocks of masonry, which have resisted the roll of this impetuous river for more than seventeen centuries, are a sight worth seeing, even at the expense of being immersed in cold water to the full extent of the lower extremities. That side of the piers which is directed towards the stream is pointed. The luis holes remain in the stones. The grooves formed for the iron rods and cramps can be discerned. The western abutment has been of the same form and construction as the other, but it is in a great measure submerged by the encroachments of the river. In favourable circumstances it can be seen from the bank. There are indications which render it probable that the western abutment, as well as the eastern, was furnished with a tower of defence. In leaving this subject, a single extract from Mr. Clayton's interesting paper may be allowed. "Those who have seen the magnificent remains of the Pont du Gard (justly the pride of Gallia Narbonensis), lighted by the glorious sun of Languedoc, may think lightly of these meagre relics of the bridge of Cilurnum, under the darker skies of Northumberland; but it may be safely affirmed, that the bridge over

The Water Piers.

Western Abutment.

the Gardon does not span a lovelier stream than the North Tyne, and that so much as remains of the masonry of the bridge of Cilurnum, leads to the conclusion that this bridge, as originally constructed, was not inferior in solidity of material, and excellency of workmanship, to the mighty structure reared by Roman hands in Gaul."

IV.—Objects of Antiquarian Interest within the Lines of the Great Barrier.

Although the pilgrim who has time at his command will not allow his attention to be diverted from his great study until he has examined it from sea to sea, others less fortunate may be obliged to take a portion only at a time, and in passing to and fro upon the railway, may be disposed to notice some of the places occurring in the route. More than one of them, moreover, are places of Roman interest. As we have now arrived at Chollerford, which has direct communication with Hexham and Newcastle by means of the Border Counties Railway, this seems to be the fitting place for introducing some memoranda respecting the towns, castles, and villages, lying within that portion of the Wall which we have already traversed. We will, as usual, proceed from east to west.

Ryton.

The village of Ryton stands high upon the south bank of the Tyne, distant about seven miles from Newcastle. The church, which is mostly of early English character, is an exceedingly favourable specimen of an English parish church. Its spire is 108 feet high, and is a conspicuous object for many miles round. On the north side of the church, shaded by trees, is a large barrow, which has not been opened. It doubtless covers the remains of some hero long departed. The views from the church-yard are both extensive and beautiful. **Ryton Church.** **Barrow.**

Prudhoe Castle.

Prudhoe Castle stands on an eminence on the south bank of the Tyne, opposite Ovingham. It is surrounded by a double ditch. The entrance gateway and the keep are Norman, being remains of the castle built by Odinel de Umfreville in the reign of Henry II. The other portions of the castle belong chiefly to the latter part of the reign of Edward I. or the beginning of that of Edward II. The oriel in the chapel over the gateway is the earliest specimen known in England. The barbican is good. Prudhoe Castle is described by Hartshorne in the *Newcastle Volumes of the Archæological Institute*, vol. ii., p. 247, and by Parker in his *Domestic Architecture of the Fourteenth Century*, p. 206. A curious bridge carries the road over the ravine south-east of the castle. "It has, we believe," says Mr. Longstaffe, "hitherto escaped observation by the writers on Prudhoe, and yet it is perhaps one of the earliest bridges in the North. It is composed of plain ribs forming a circular arch, but the end or front arches are pointed, forming a most picturesque assemblage." **Early Oriel.** **Ancient Bridge.**

(*Archæologia Æliana*, N. S., vol. vi., p. 121.)

Ovingham.

On the north bank of the river, immediately opposite to Prudhoe, is the pretty village of Ovingham. A ferry-boat is the usual mode of transit. The church, which is of early English character, has lately been carefully SaxonTower. restored. The tower is one of the few in England that has any claims to be reputed Saxon; the baluster-windows in the belfry are characteristic. Here, before the Reformation, was a cell for three black canons, subject to the Priory of Hexham. The present parsonage house occupies the site of it. "The little square decorated window of two trefoiled lights is fairly attributed to the oratory of the masters of the cell. The door Door-rasp. of the parsonage has in lieu of a knocker the old *door-rasp*, now nearly extinct in England." (*Arch. Æl.*, N.S., vol. v., Bewick. p. 124.) Bewick, the wood-engraver, lies in the churchyard. He was born at Cherry-burn House, on the opposite side of the river, in 1753.

Corbridge.

The Roman station of CORSTOPITUM must have been an important one, standing as it did upon the Watling Street, and commanding the passage of the Tyne. The station, which is now entirely uprooted, was to the west of the present town. Its site, which is raised a little above the Corchester. general level, is called Corchester. When the water of the river is low and clear, the remains of the Roman bridge (particularly on the south side) may be seen. A defaced altar and other minor memorials of Roman occupation are to be met with in the town. The church is almost wholly built of Roman stones. Inserted in its north wall is a stone having rudely sculptured on it a boar, the emblem of the 20th legion. The celebrated Corbridge Lanx—a silver sacrificing dish of the Roman period—is in the possession of the Duke of Northumberland. It was found here in 1735. Hard by the church is a peel-tower, once the residence of the vicars. Mr. Hartshorne says, "It is remarkable for the perfect state of the interior, which shews the whole of the domestic arrangements peculiar to that time." He is of opinion that it must have been built during the reign of Edward II., at the time the manor belonged to Henry, first Lord Percy of Alnwick. (*Newcastle Volumes of Arch. Inst*, vol. ii., p. 79.)

The Lanx.

The Peel.

Aydon Castle.

Aydon Castle is little more than a mile and a half from Corbridge, in the direction of Halton Castle, and the Roman Wall. It is a remarkably perfect specimen of a fortified hall, dating from the latter part of the 13th century. It is described and very abundantly illustrated in the *Domestic Architecture of the Middle Ages*, vol. i., p. 148. The chief entrance is yet by an external flight of steps; the stable is evidently contrived for the preservation of cattle from an assault; no wood is used in its construction, even its mangers being of stone. Amongst other details, a good example of a drain will be noticed, and an external chimney

Dilston Hall.

Dilston Hall stands upon an eminence skirted by the Devil's Water, not far from the confluence of that stream with the Tyne. A more picturesque situation can scarcely be conceived. William, son of Aluric, was Lord of Dilston in the 17th of Henry VII. Sir Francis Radcliffe, who married a natural daughter of Charles II., was created Earl of Derwentwater by James II. James, "the unfortunate Earl of Derwentwater," was a grandson of the first earl. He was a man "of an amiable disposition, he exercised an almost princely liberality, and he was regarded with affectionate veneration by men of every rank." He entered most reluctantly into the rebellion of 1715, and was beheaded on Tower Hill, 23 Feb., 1716. His estates were forfeited to the crown, and are now held by the Commissioners of the Greenwich Hospital. Dilston Hall, which was erected by Francis Radcliffe, in 1616, seems to have been a spacious and elegant structure. After the execution of the Earl, it was allowed to fall into decay, and was eventually removed. A portion of the old tower of the Devilstones, which had been incorporated with the more modern hall, remains. A handsome bridge of a single arch spans the rivulet, which led to the deer park. An avenue of noble horse-chestnut trees marks the approach to the mansion. A small chapel stands hard by, in the vault of which lie the remains of several of the Derwentwater family. The vault was opened in 1805. The body of the last earl was examined. It was found to have been embalmed; the head lying by the body, with the marks of the

The Derwentwater Family.

The Vault.

axe clearly discernible; the hair was perfect, the features were regular and wearing the appearance of youth. A blacksmith getting access to the vault, extracted several of the Earl's teeth, which he sold for a half-a-crown a piece; and which multiplied exceedingly, as the demand for them grew. Demand and Supply. A much-weathered Roman monumental slab is inserted in one of the buildings. There is an excellent paper on Dilston Hall, in *Howitt's Visits to Remarkable Places*, second series, from the pen of a lady, whose decease all who knew her mourn —Mrs. Grey, the lady of John Grey, Esq., of Dilston Hall.

The modern mansion on the brink of the Devil's Water, has been erected for the residence of the agent of the Commissioners of the Greenwich Hospital in the North.

Hexham.

The appearance of Hexham from the railway is very picturesque. Of Roman Origin. This is no doubt the site of a Roman station, but its Roman designation has not been satisfactorily ascertained. Stukeley says, "This town was undoubtedly Roman; we judged the *castrum* was where the castellated building now stands, east of the market place, which is the brow of the hill, and has a good prospect." About the year 674 Bishop Wilfred built a church here. Wilfred's Church. In 680 Hexham was raised to the dignity of an episcopal see, an honour which it retained, under a succession of twelve bishops, until A.D. 821. The only portion of Wilfred's building that remains is the crypt; the church itself seems to have been laid in ruins by the Danes in 867, in which state it long continued. Priory Church. The present church is an exceedingly beautiful specimen of the early English style. It was probably erected at the close of the twelfth or beginning of the thirteenth century. The nave was destroyed during an incursion of the Scots in 1296, and it has never been rebuilt. The chancel has recently been repaired and refitted with considerable care. The eastern termination has been entirely rebuilt. The Lady Chapel, which was of late decorated work, being in an exceedingly dilapidated condition, has been removed. This church had the privilege of sanctuary. The Saxon frid-stool, or seat of safety, is preserved in the church. One of the peculiar features of the church, and one which is coeval with the building, is a massive staircase at the end of the south transept. It leads to a platform, which has three door-ways; one going up to the bell-tower, another taking to the scriptorium over the chapter-house (the same as at Furness Abbey), and another leading to the relic and plate closet over the groined passage proceeding from the cloisters to the south side of the chancel. Mr. Longstaffe has thrown out the idea, which is exceedingly probable, that in this part of the church persons claiming the right of sanctuary were accommodated. The chancel is the earliest part of the church, and is is exceedingly light and elegant. The rood-screen, which of the later perpendicular style, will attract attention. It is covered with paintings; amongst them being several of the subjects of "The Dance of Death." In the church are preserved, though not in their original situation, the shrine of Prior Rowland Lechman, who ruled the convent between 1479 and 1499, and the tomb of Robert Ogle, who died in 1410. In the north transept is a cross-legged effigy, which is probably that of Gilbert de Umfreville, who died in 1307. Beside this effigy are two others of nearly

The Frid-Stool.

Monumental Effigies.

the same date. One is that of a lady with a wimple. The other is the figure of a knight, who, from his heraldic bearings—three garbs on a fess—is supposed to be one of the family of Aydon.

Some remains of the chapter-house, or of a vestibule leading into it, may be seen on the east of the south transept. The cloister garth lay on the south of the nave. At the west end of it is a rich and beautiful arcade of the early decorated period. Chapter House.

The prior's house has been almost entirely rebuilt, and is now used as a private dwelling. The north gateway of the priory (Gilligate) remains, though in a ruinous condition. It possesses one peculiar feature. In front of the gate has been a vaulted portico, where a mounted messenger might await communications with the prior. Local tradition has it, that the last of the priors was hung over his own porch; the probability, however, is that his execution took place at Tyburn. Prior's House.

The gateway tower, on the east side of the market-place, is a building of great beauty. The Courts of the Manor of Hexham are still held in it. The large square tower on the hill seems to have been the stronghold of the place. Its walls are nine feet thick; it has two vaulted dungeons. Its projecting battlements have a very fine effect. It is now used as the manor office. Castellated Remains.

We now revert to the crypt. It was accidently discovered in the early part of the last century. After being almost forgotten, attention was again called to it by Mr. Fairless, in the second volume of the *Journal of the Archæological Institute.* A similar crypt exists at Ripon, The Crypt.

where Wilfred also built a church. It is entirely built of Roman stones. The use of its various parts is quite a mystery. Mr. Fairless says, "There have been three approaches to this solemn and drear retreat, one of them at present reaching nearly into the body of the church; another, to the south, leading to the cloisters; the third rising into the nave." The wood-cut represents one of its passages.

The present entrance is by a ladder, from the church-yard. Besides some exceedingly graceful mouldings and devices, which were afterwards adopted by the Gothic artists, two

Roman inscriptions have been built up into the crypt. One of them is too imperfect to be deciphered; the other is shown in the cut. Inscriptions.

It records the names of Septimius Severus (who assumed the name of his predecesor, Pertinax), and of his son Caracalla, who took the style of Aurelius Antoninus. The name of his other son, Geta, has been obliterated. The third and fourth lines of the inscription probably stood thus:—

. . ET IMP. P. SEP.
GETA COHORTES.

Certain cohorts and vexillations seem to have been employed upon some work at this time; what, does not appear.

Large find of Saxon Stycas.

In the year 1832 the sexton, when digging a grave deeper than usual, on the west side of the north transept of the church, struck upon a vessel of Saxon workmanship, containing, it is calculated, about eight thousand Saxon coins.

These proved to be *stycas*, a small coin peculiar to Northumberland. The remains of the vessel, with about 300 of the coins, were transmitted to the British Museum. Mr. Fairless, who for half a century has, with kindly and enlightened zeal, trimmed the lamp of antiquarian lore in this favoured seat of Roman, Saxon, and monastic magnificence, is the fortunate possessor of nearly a thousand choice specimens. The coins are about half an inch in diameter, composed of a mixture of metals nearly resembling the Corinthian brass of the ancients. They are most beautifully executed, the letters being sharper and better formed than those on the Norman and Plantagenet series. The coins belong to a period extending from A.D. 790 to A.D. 844. Probably this hoard was concealed in prospect of the Danish invasion. *See A Guide to the Abbey Church*, by Joseph Fairless; *Account of Anglo-Saxon Stycas*, by Mr. Adamson, in *Arch. Æl.*, O. S., vol. iii., p. 77, &c.; *Roman Hexham, Arch. Æl.*, N. S., vol. v., 145; *Hexham Church*, by Mr. Longstaffe, *ibid.* p. 150.

V. From the Tyne to the Tipalt.

We resume our mural investigations at the point where we discontinued them — the inn at Chollerford. A walk of a little more than half a mile along the turnpike road, which is here made pleasant with trees of vigorous growth, brings us from Chollerford to Chesters, the seat of John Clayton, Esq. Within the grounds are the station of Cilurnum, some fragments of the Wall, and a collection of antiquities of peculiar interest.

Cilurnum—Chesters.

In passing from the house to the station, the position of the Wall may be noticed; the path-way lies in the north fosse. Although the station has doubtless contributed its proportion of stones to the construction of the neighbouring mansion, and although its position in the park must have led to the levelling of its surface, its form is still quite distinct. The station is a large one, having an area of five acres and a quarter. A portion of the west wall of the station, near its northern extremity, and its south-west angle, have been cleared of the accumulated rubbish in order to display the masonry. All the gateways of the station may be discerned. The northern and eastern have been excavated; the others, shew themselves by the dip in the line of rampart. The northern gateway is not in a good state of preservation. The foundation of the pillar which divided it into two portals remains, and there are some traces of an advanced work on its eastern side. The eastern gate — leading to the bridge — is in a better state. The sockets in which the pivots of the folding doors moved, and the central stone against which they struck when closed, will be noticed. There are also the remains of the guard chambers on each side. It is rather remarkable that this gateway is a single one. At Housesteads, we shall find that all the gateways have originally consisted of two portals, each being closed with two-leaved gates. Traces of the road leading from this gate to the river, may be noticed. The Wall, which has come up from the river's brink, has struck the station a little to the north of this gateway. A portion of it has

Description of the Station.

been laid bare; it is 7 feet 6 inches thick, and it exhibits on its south side five courses of facing-stones. A range of buildings within the eastern rampart of the station was excavated by Mr. Clayton, in 1843. Although the frosts and rains of twenty winters have taken some effect upon the ruins, they will well repay the minute attention of the antiquary. An account of the excavations, from the pen of Mr. Clayton, will be found in *Archæologia Æliana*, O.S., vol. iii., p. 142. The points to which the attention of the observer may most advantageously be directed are the narrowness of the streets, the mode in which the hanging floors or hypocausts have been constructed, and the extent to which the steps and the doorways of some of the chambers have been worn away by the tread of feet. The building nearest the river has evidently been a place of public resort. If the pillars supporting the broken floor of concrete be examined, it will be seen that some of them are the shafts of columns which have no doubt occupied a more honourable position in some previously existing building. The furnace which supplied these chambers with heated air stood near the southern extremity of the excavation; but the tiles composing it, as well as the stone pillars in its vicinity, having been strongly acted on by fire, have crumbled into a shapeless mass. One of the chambers of this building, on its northern side, contained a bath formed by drawing a dwarf wall of Roman tiles across the room. When discovered, the bath was carefully lined with red cement, which, from the action of the weather, has peeled off. The wall forming the end and one side of the bath has, from the same cause, been thrown into disorder. The excellency of

The Baths.

The Furnace.

the masonry of some parts of this building will strike the observer. Until quite recently the marks of the trowel in finishing the joints of the courses were apparent. The woodcut represents a buttress at the north-east angle of the build-

ing. These ruined walls are the favourite habitat of many wild plants of great beauty and some rarity. It is interesting to see life, fragrance, and grace, springing from the grave of empire.

A vaulted chamber, somewhat nearer the centre of the Ærarium.
station than the "baths," will next attract the attention of the pilgrim. A tradition has long prevailed that an underground stable existed in the vicinity of the camp capable of containing five hundred horses. When this chamber was struck upon, the workmen thought that the statements of their "fore-elders" were about to be verified.

An oaken door, bound and studded with iron, closed the entrance into the chamber, but it fell to pieces shortly after being exposed. On the floor were found a number of base denarii, chiefly of the reign of Severus; hence the conclusion was drawn that the chamber constituted the Ærarium or Treasury of the station. The roof of the apartment is peculiar. It consists of three separate arches, the intervals between them being filled up by the process called "stepping over."

No other buildings are left exposed in the station, though wherever the surface is removed Roman masonry is found. A sward of unusual richness covers the city which for several centuries gave to Rome the command of the valley of the North Tyne.

Suburban buildings have left their traces between the station and the river, and ruins more extensive than usual are spread over the ground to the south. No habitations have been erected to the north of the station, or the Wall.

The burying ground of the station was to the south of it, at a point where the river bends rapidly to the east, and where the sunk fence defining the park of Chesters joins the river's bank. This fact has been inferred from the number of monumental slabs that have been found here. Burying ground of the Station.

CILURNUM was garrisoned by the second ala of Astures —a people from the modern Asturia, in Spain.

Several important inscriptions, sculptures, and other relics of the Roman era, found in the station and its vicinity, are preserved at Chesters. To a few of these the attention of the pilgrim is directed. A stone lintel, here represented, has in bold relief two sea-monsters, the emblems, no doubt, of the second legion. The usual badges of this legion are Inscriptions and Sculptures.

a sea-goat and Pegasus; the place of Pegasus seems in this instance to have been taken by a second marine animal.

The most important inscription records the dedication to Marcus Aurelius [Elagabalus] and his intended successor [Severus Alexander] of some building which, having decayed through age, had been restored by the second ala of Astures. This dedication took place on the 30th October, in the consulship of Gratus and Seleucus, A.D. 221. The inscription is shewn below.

J STOREY DEL. R UTTING SC

The River-god Tyne.

A figure, slightly mutilated, and shewn below, was found in the building near the east gateway. It is believed to represent the genius of the North Tyne.

Cybele.

A mutilated, but very graceful figure, was found in the

J. STOREY, del. UTTING, sc.

south-west corner of the station. It is believed to represent Cybele, the mother of the gods, and is here figured. The border of her tunic is of a tasteful design. She stands upon an animal which is no doubt intended for a bull. The statue is made of fine-grained sandstone, and is about six feet high. It is seldom that statues of so large a size occur in Roman stations in Britain. The drawing on the next page represents a group of stones found in the station or its vicinity. The composite capital enables us to form an idea of the ornate character of some of the buildings of the station. The stones by its side are of the kind called centurial. One of them indicates that the part of the Wall in which it was inserted was built by the century or troop of one hundred men, commanded by Valerius Maximus; the other by the century of Rufus Sabinus. Several pipes formed of clay, and evi-

Mater Deorum.

Centurial Stones.

dently intended for the conveyance of water, have been found at this and other stations. One is shewn in the cut.

The Border-counties Railway, shortly after crossing the Tyne, cuts through an excellent bed of clay, previously unknown, but which, there is reason to suppose, was used by the Romans.

Departure from Chesters.

Leaving the garden at Chesters, and proceeding along the plantation which lies to the west of the house, we meet with a piece of the Wall, covered with honey-suckle and other plants, and presenting four courses of facing-stones in position. The fosse behind it is used as a duck-pond.

Beyond this, the foundation of the Wall forms the slightly elevated crown of a path leading through the plantation. The fosse is on the right hand.

Emerging from the grounds of Chesters, we are once more upon the turnpike road, and climb the hill which leads to Walwick. The lines of the Vallum are seen in the field on the left. A fine ash-tree is growing on the north agger. The foundations of the Wall are often seen in the road. The wood-cut here introduced was prepared under unusually favourable circumstances; no new "metal" had for long been

Foundations of the Wall.

placed on the road, and recent thunder-showers had removed all dust. The large house on the top of the hill was formerly an inn. In front of the cottage, just beyond, is a slight elevation, probably caused by the remains of a mile-castle. The view from Walwick is exceedingly fine, commanding as it does the vales of Tyne, Warden Hill,

Walwick.

WardenHill. the hill behind Wall (both of which have been fortified by the Ancient Britons), and Hexham, with its Abbey Church, beautiful even in the distance. After passing Walwick, the turnpike road leaves the Wall, and runs by the side of the Vallum; the fosse of the Wall is on our right.

Tower Taye. Ascending the next hill, called Tower Taye, we come to a small tower, built, about a century ago, out of the stones of the Wall. Reaching the summit of the hill, all the lines of the Barrier come grandly into view. Proceeding onwards, we find, on the right, the remains of a mile-castle very distinctly marked. On the hill to the left of us are some ancient quarries. To the south of the quarries, and nearly opposite

Temporary camp. the mile-castle, is an earthen entrenchment, the gateways of which are furnished with traverses. It was no doubt occupied by the Romans when the Wall was in course of construction. The road now runs upon the north agger of the Vallum, which has been spread out to form it. A very fine piece of Wall, six feet high, is seen on our right, running

Black-Carts Farm. along the Black-carts farm. The fosse of the Vallum is also exceedingly good. On the top of the next hill, Limestone Bank, several things demand our attention. The view to the north is fine, embracing the valley of the North Tyne, with Chipchase Castle on its north bank, and the Simonside and Cheviot Hills in the distance. A castellum, with which the stone dikes of the fields unfortunately interfere, is on the summit. Here we, for the first time, meet with a

Military Way. piece of the military way which accompanied the Wall throughout its entire length. It is seen coming up to the south gateway of the castellum; and then, bending away from it, proceeds on its westwards course. The road has un-

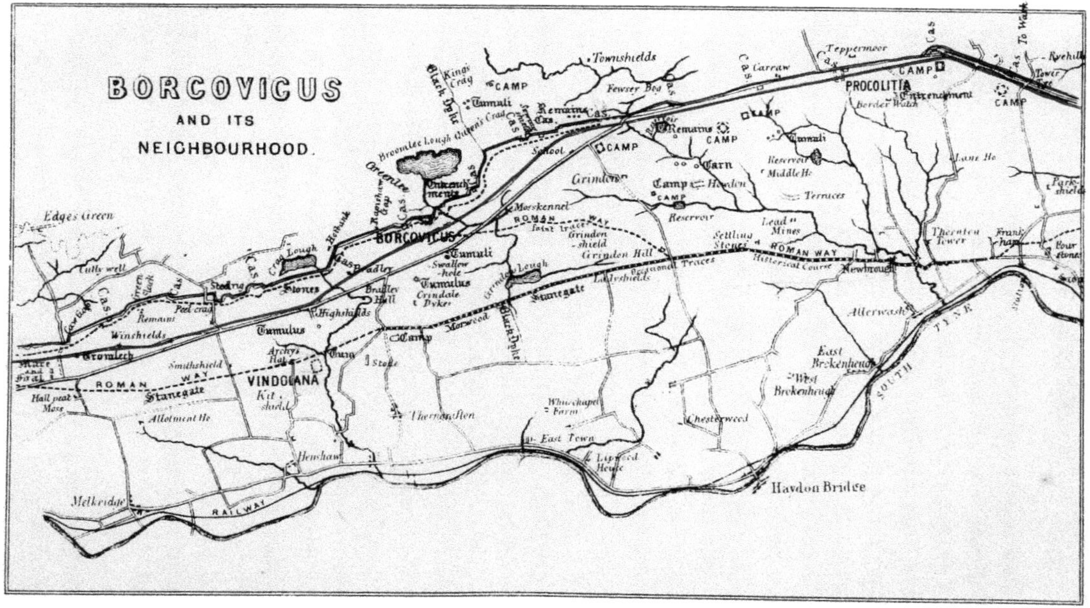
BORCOVICUS
AND ITS
NEIGHBOURHOOD.
BORCOVICUS
VINDOLANA
PROCOLITIA
ROMAN WAY
Stanegate
Townshields
Fewser Bog
Remains
Cas.
CAMP
Tumuli
Tumulus
Grindon
Grinden Hill
Moskennel
School
Teppermoor
Carraw
Border Watch
Entrenchment
Reservoir
Middle Ho
Terraces
Lead Mines
Settling Stones
Newbrough
Allerwash
East Brokenheugh
West Brokenheugh
Chesterweed
Whitechapel Farm
East Town
Haydon Bridge
SOUTH TYNE
Henshaw
Melkridge
RAILWAY
Allotment Ho
Thornghafton
Edges Green
Cully well
Winshields
Peel crag
Crag Lough
Highshields
Bradley Hall
Grindale Dyker
Swallow hole
Black Dyke
Morwood
Camp
Occasional Traces
Historical Course
Thornton Tower
Lane Ho
Lady's shields
Hall peat Moss
Broomlee Lough
Greenlee
Kings Crag
Queen's Crag
Entrenchments
Hotbank
Rapishaw Gap
Stone
Kit shield
Archy's Hall
Smithshield
Carn
Camp
To Wark
Ryehill
Tower Tye
Four Stones
Park shield

fortunately been largely robbed in order to supply material for building the stone fences.

The fosse both of Wall and Vallum may next be examined. In each case it has been cut through the basalt which forms the summit of the hill; and the excavated masses lie upon its brink. How the Romans managed to dislodge such large blocks of this tough material without the aid of gunpowder is a marvel. Dr. Lingard, in his MS. *Tourification of the Wall*, says—"It is a most astonishing sight." South of the plantation, on the summit of the hill, and nearly opposite the castellum, is another temporary camp. Its entrenchments, its gateways, and traverses are all visible.

The ditch cut through "whin."

Temporary camp.

Proceeding onwards, we come to the farm-house of Carrawburgh. The farm-house on our right hand is called Teppermoor. Just after passing a small quarry on our left, we come to the remains of another mile-castle, and immediately after that we encounter the station of PROCOLITIA.

Carrawburgh.

Procolitia,—Carrawburgh.

The site of this station is all desolation, but the aspect of its herbage indicates the usual richness of a Roman camp. It is about three miles and a half from Cilurnum, and it contains an area of about three acres and a half. It was garrisoned by the first cohort of Batavians. This fact is brought out in the mutilated stone, shown in the woodcut on the next page, and which was found here. The date of this inscription is A.D. 237, when Maximinus was emperor, and Perpetuus and Cornelianus were consuls. The Batavians and their neighbours

Its situation.

First cohort of Batavians.

in the next station, the Tungrians, seem to have been in Britain for a very long time. Tacitus tells us that Agricola commenced the battle of the Grampians by ordering three Batavian and two Tungrian cohorts to charge the enemy sword in hand. The ramparts of this station are distinct, and, if freed from rubbish, would be found to stand several feet high. The position of the east, south, and west gateways are clearly discernible. The great Wall has coalesced with the north rampart of the station. Outside the western wall are distinct marks of suburban buildings. A natural valley, permeated by a stream of water,

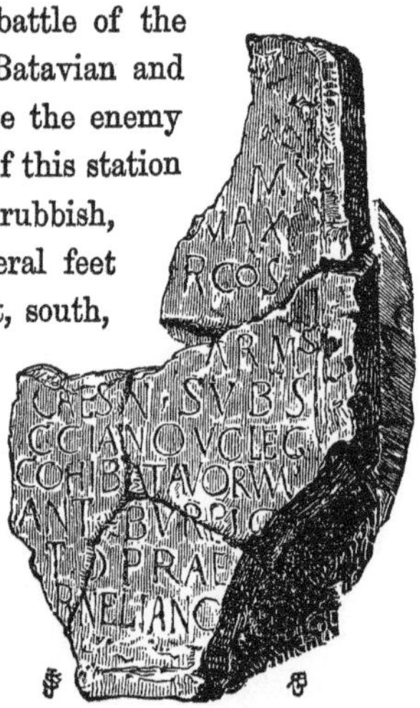

gives strength to the fortification on this side. In Horsley's day a well was noticed here, cased with masonry. "The people called it a cold bath, and rightly judged it to be Roman." Passing onwards, we soon reach the farm-house of Carraw, formerly a rural retreat of the Priors of Hexham. We soon pass the site of another castellum. To the south of the Wall in this vicinity is an earthen camp, which commands an extensive prospect; it is called Brown-Dikes. On the top of the next hill the works approach very close to each other; the Vallum proceeds onwards in a straight line, but the Wall swerves towards it for the double purpose (apparently) of avoiding a bog on the north, and securing the crown of the hill.

Carraw.

BrownDikes.

Another mile-castle is passed on our right hand, and shortly afterwards we have the cottage of Shield-on-the-Wall on our left. The sheet of water below is an artificial accumulation, for the purpose of supplying the Settlingstones Lead-mines. The bold basaltic ridge along which the Wall runs now comes strongly into view. Four great mountain waves are before us — the escarpments of the strata—which seem to chase each other, to the north. We now, to adopt the language of Hutton, "quit the beautiful scenes of cultivation, and enter upon the rude of nature and the wreck of antiquity." Shield on the Wall.

After passing the 27th mile-stone, the modern military road takes to the south of both Vallum and Wall. The Wall and Vallum also part company, the Wall taking to the heights, and adhering most tenaciously to every projecting headland; the Vallum, on the other hand, running along the "tail" of the hill. Their respective distance is continually varying. We are now at Sewingshields. XXVII miles.

Langley Castle and Smelt-Mills.—Chesterwood.

As many pilgrims will approach Sewingshields from Haydon Bridge; or, after a day's toil upon the crags, may resort thither to obtain a night's repose, a brief digression is here required. In the village itself there is little to attract the attention of the stranger. About a mile and a half to the south of it is Langley Castle, a ruin which presents features of very considerable interest. It consists of an oblong building, strengthened at each corner by a strong square tower. In addition to those towers, is another containing a circular staircase leading to each story. Another digression. Langley Castle.

The door is protected by a portcullis. A vaulted recess is hard by, in which a mounted messenger might take shelter. The building belongs to the latter half of the fourteenth century. Its roof and internal fittings were destroyed by fire at an early but unascertained period. Its masonry is still exceedingly good. The wood-cut exhibits

Destroyed by Fire.

its general appearance. The most remarkable feature of the building is its garderobes. The whole of the south-west tower is given up to them. On each of the three floors there are four placed in recessed arches. They communicate, by means of flues, with a pit below, through which a stream of water was turned. This series of arcades has a singular and handsome appearance. The Barony of Langley became in 1383 the possession of Henry Percy, Earl of Northumberland, when, by reason of his

Its series of Arcades.

marriage with Maud, heiress of Antony Lord Lucy, and widow of Gilbert de Umfreville, the large possessions of the Umfrevilles and Lucys became united with those of the Percys. Langley was the property of the Earl of Derwentwater at the time of his unhappy rebellion. It now belongs to the Greenwich Hospital. As we walk along the wall-crowned heights we shall keep Langley Castle long in view. For a description of Langley Castle, see *Domestic Arch. Middle Ages*, xiv. cent., pp. 113, 332.

A little beyond Langley Castle are the Langley Smelt-mills, where the lead-ore procured in the district is reduced. Within a mile of the small market town of Allendale is another establishment for the same purpose, and a third, some miles further south, at Allenheads. Formerly the fumes from the furnaces were taken direct to the chimneys. As a good deal of lead in a volatilised state is brought away by the draught, much property was lost, deleterious matter was diffused in the air and deposited in the fields; and, as a necessary consequence, the health of the workmen was injured, and cattle and sheep were occasionally poisoned. Now, however, the vapours are taken along flues laid on the ground, and they eventually discharge themselves by a chimney planted upon the top of a hill at the distance, it may be, of two or three miles from the works. The consequence of this arrangement is, that the metallic particles of the vapour are deposited before it reaches the outlet. In connection with the three smelt-mills belonging to Mr. Beaumont there are nine miles of flue; the sweeping of them once a year brings in a joyous harvest of from six to ten thousand

Lead smelt-mills.

The fumes of the lead condensed.

pounds. As we walk along the mural heights we shall see the chimney stalks of some of these smelt-mills.

We now return to Haydon Bridge. Sewingshields, where the Wall begins to climb the heights, is about five miles distant, in a northerly direction. As the road is nearly one continuous ascent, the pilgrim must prepare for a considerable expenditure of muscular energy.

Chesterwood.

A little to the north of Haydon Bridge, and somewhat to the left of the direct road leading to Sewingshields, is the village of Chesterwood. The name indicates a place of strength. Whilst the Lords of the Marches reared for themselves castles like Langley, the commonalty took refuge in a class of fortified dwellings called Peel Houses.

Peels.

These consisted of strong buildings, having one apartment on the ground floor, and another above it. The upper room was approached by a flight of steps. At night the cattle belonging to the farmer were secured in the apartment below, whilst he and his family barricaded themselves in the room above. This upper room was floored with stone flags, resting upon heavy oak-beams, which would long resist the action of fire. The gray slates of the roof, were pinned down with sheep's shanks. Arrow loops were placed in various parts of the building, so as to expose an enemy to the utmost disadvantage. Chesterwood seems to have consisted of a congeries of these little fortresses. In the moss-trooping times the inhabitants found it necessary to cluster together for their mutual safety. Now they place houses wherever convenience dictates. Hence (although our rural population is diminishing), a deserted hamlet must not always be taken as a sign of depopulation.

The wood-cut shows two of the peel-houses of Chesterwood. The house on the right hand has had the stairs of entrance

removed. Since the wood-cut was prepared, the other house has become untenanted, and is at present in a very dilapidated condition; it nods to its fall.

Leaving Chesterwood and arriving at Grindonhill farm-house, we cross the direct Roman road which runs from Chesters to Carvoran. It is here called the Causeway; elsewhere it is called the Stanegate. As it has for centuries been used as a common road, and has been often repaired, it has lost much of its Roman character. Grindonhill.

On reaching the modern military road, we have Sewingshields farm-house, and the mural heights, directly before us. A modest building by the side of the road will be noticed. This is the school-house of the district. Here for quarter of a century Mr. Adam Cranston moulded with a skill and kindness all his own the minds of the youth of the mural district. Long may he enjoy his present dignified ease.

Sewing-shields.

We now take the Wall at the point where it begins to ascend the hill. On the ascent to Sewingshields farm-house it has been rooted up within a recent period to furnish building stones for the enlargement of the house, and the construction of fences. When Dr. Lingard passed this way, in 1807, he found the Wall five feet high. The fosse as it begins to ascend the hill, is good, but on reaching the mile-castle it altogether dies away, the height of the cliff rendering it unnecessary. The interior of the mile-castle is planted with trees. On the moor, opposite to it (south of the modern road), is another of those temporary camps, of which we have had so many examples. North of the Wall are two works of interest. One of them seems to belong to the ancient British period. It is opposite the mile-castle. It consists of a slightly elevated platform of a somewhat trapezoidal shape, surrounded by a well defined ditch. In one direction this camp measures 105 feet, in another 94 feet. Within its area are some of those rounded forms, which are supposed to be indicative of the dwellings of our rude ancestors. At the northern extremity of this little encampment, and inclosed within the general rampart, is a circular space, depressed below the general level. It is forty-eight feet in diameter; and may have been formed for cattle. This small encampment has a weak and defenceless aspect at present; but when the whole waste was a morass, or a forest, it would be comparatively sheltered and secure. To the west of this, and in a direction nearly north-east from the farm-house, is the site of Sewingshields

Temporary Camp.

British earth-work.

Castle, referred to by Sir Walter Scott in the sixth canto of Harold the Dauntless, under the denomination of the Castle of the Seven Shields. Too truly he says :— The Castle.

> . . . . "No towers are seen
> On the wild heath, but those that Fancy builds,
> And, save a fosse that tracks the moor with green,
> Is nought remains to tell of what may there have been."

When Dr. Lingard was here, its walls were five feet high. The present farm tenant, Mr. Errington (a succourer of pilgrims), removed the vaults of the castle. It stood in the centre of the only patch of ground in "the moss," which is now subjected to the plough. There are traces of what seem to be two fish-ponds on its northern margin.

But though the walls of the castle have been uprooted, the following tradition relating to it will not readily perish :— Tradition of King Arthur.

"Immemorial tradition has asserted, that King Arthur, his queen Guenever, his court of lords and ladies, and his hounds, were enchanted in some cave of the crags, or in a hall below the castle of Sewingshields, and would continue entranced there till some one should first blow a bugle-horn that lay on a table near the entrance of the hall, and then with 'the sword of the stone' cut a garter also placed there beside it. But none had ever heard where the entrance to this enchanted hall was, till the farmer at Sewingshields, about fifty years since, was sitting knitting on the ruins of the castle, and his clew fell, and ran downwards through a rush of briars and nettles, as he supposed, into a deep subterranean passage. Full in the faith that the entrance into King Arthur's hall was now discovered, he cleared the briary portal of its weeds and rubbish, and entering a vaulted passage, followed, in his darkling way, the thread of his clew. The floor was infested with toads and lizards; and the dark wings of bats, disturbed by his unhallowed intrusion, flitted fearfully around him. At length his sinking courage was strengthened by a dim, distant light, which, as he advanced grew gradually brighter, till, all at once, he entered a vast and vaulted hall, in the centre of which, a fire without fuel, from a broad crevice in the floor, blazed with a high and lambent flame, that shewed all the carved walls and fretted roof, and the monarch and his queen and court, reposing around in a theatre of thrones and costly couches. On the floor, beyond the fire, lay the faithful and deep-toned pack of thirty couple of hounds; and on a table before it, the spell-dissolving horn, sword, and garter. The shepherd reverently, but firmly, grasped the sword, and as he drew it leisurely from its rusty scabbard, the eyes of the monarch, and his courtiers began to open, and they rose till they sat upright. He cut the garter; and as the sword was being slowly sheathed, the spell assumed its ancient power, and they all gradually sunk to rest; but not before the monarch had lifted up his eyes and hands, and exclaimed:

O woe betide that evil day
On which this witless wight was born,
Who drew the sword—the garter cut,
But never blew the bugle-horn.

Terror brought on loss of memory, and the shepherd was unable to give any correct account of his adventure, or to find again the entrance to the enchanted hall."—*Hodgson's Northumberland*, II., iii., 287.

The King and Queen's Crags.

One more local tradition of this renowned king, the pilgrim may be pleased to hear, as he may personally verify it:—To the north of Sewingshields, two strata of sandstone crop out to the day; the highest points of each ledge are called the King and Queen's-crag, from the following legend. King Arthur, seated on the farthest rock, was talking with his queen, who, meanwhile, was engaged in arranging her 'back hair.' Some expression of the queen's having offended his majesty, he seized a rock which lay near him, and, with an exertion of strength for which the Picts were proverbial, threw it at her, a distance of about a quarter of a mile! The queen with great dexterity, caught it upon her comb, and thus warded off the blow; the stone fell between them, where it lies to this very day, with the marks of the comb upon it, to attest the truth of the story. It probably weighs about twenty tons!

The farm-house of Sewingshields is entirely built out of the stones of the Wall. Its kindly occupants have lived to see their children's grandchildren, and can tell of times and of traditions that are fast wending to oblivion. A centurial stone is built up in front of the gig-house here. It may probably be read—The century of Gellius Philippus [erected this part of the Wall.]

From Sewingshields to Carvoran the Roman military way, which accompanied the Wall throughout its entire length, is, with but few intermissions, to be seen. It is always to the south of the Wall, but does not keep parallel with it; it selects the easiest gradients. As we approach the mural ridge from the south, its course can generally be detected by the peculiar tint of its herbage. Military way.

We now pursue our course westwards. For a little distance we go through a young plantation. The basaltic columns soon attract attention. There used to be one that was dignified with the name of King Arthur's Chair, but it was purposely thrown down. Every thunder-storm dislodges some. We soon come to Cat's Gate, a narrow chasm in the rocks, by which, according to tradition, the Scots crept under the Wall; it has an artificial appearance. A mile-castle is next reached. It has been much robbed lately for the repairs of the farm-house. Broomlee Lake, to the north of the Wall, now comes boldly into view. According to tradition, a box of treasure lies sunk in it.—*Richardson's Table Book, Legendary Division*, v. iii., p. 100. The small sheet of water to the south of the turnpike road is Grindon Lough. Cat's Gate.

Busy Gap.

Busy Gap, one of the widest of the gaps or breaks in the basaltic chain over which the Wall runs, is the next point to be reached. Before descending into it, it will be well, from the elevated position where we now are, to pay some attention to an ancient cutting belonging to these parts, which is called the Black Dike. It consists simply of a ditch with the earth taken out of it thrown on the east side. In the old maps of Northumberland it is represented as extending from the north-west extremity of Northumberland to the Tyne at Water House, near Bardon Mill; it re-appears at Morley, and is said to go by Allenheads, into the county of Durham. We see from the height on which we stand a plantation on the other side of the valley, to the south of us, called the "Black Dike Planting." The fosse, even at this distance, may be discerned on the west side of it. The point where the Dike crossed the Wall has long been a matter of speculation. It probably crossed at the opening, west of Busy-gap, and then, as the Wall here is running in a northerly direction, it took the course which the Wall now does as far as the foot of the Sewingshields Crags; it then made off to the northern wastes, passing the Queen's and King's Crag. The Wall has destroyed all trace of it, where the course of the two structures coincided, but there are some remains of it north of Sewingshields Crag. The stone dike which forms the western boundary of the Sewingshields property probably represents it course. (*McLauchlan's Memoir*, pp. 37*n*, 42.)

The Black Dike.

After this digression, we now descend into Busy-gap. It is supposed to have got its name from the fact of its being the pass most frequented by the freebooters of the middle age. In consequonce of its width, the Roman engineers have defended it with peculiar care. In addition to the fosse on the north of the Wall, which here re-appears, a triangular rampart beyond it embraces the valley, and still further strengthens the fortification. This rampart is double on the west side.

Additional defences.

This part of the country long retained the disorganization produced by the incessant wars between England and Scotland. A "Busy-gap rogue," was a well-known name of reproach. When Camden and Cotton visited the Wall in 1599, they durst not venture into these parts. "From thence [Carvoran]," Camden says, "the Wall goeth forward more aslope by Iverton, Forsten, and Chester-in-the-Wall, [Housesteads], near to Busy-gap,—a place infamous for thieving and robbing; where stood some castles, (chesters they called them), as I heard, but I could not with safety take the full survey of it, for the rank robbers thereabouts." At a later period, 1649, Gray, in his *Chorographia*, says:—

The manners of the ancient Borderers.

"There is many Dales, the chief are Tinedale and Reedsdale, a country that William the Conqueror did not subdue, retaining to this day the ancient Laws and Customs, (according to the county of Kent) whereby the lands of the father is equally divided at his death amongst all his sonnes. These Highlanders are famous for theeving, they are all bred up and live by theft. They come down from these Dales into the low Countries, and carry away horses and cattell, so cunningly, that it will be hard for any to get them, or their cattell, except they be acquainted with some Master Thiefe; who for some mony (which they call Saufey mony) may help they to their stoln goods, or deceive them. There is many every year brought in of them into the Goale of Newcastle, and at the Assises are condemned and hanged, sometimes twenty or thirty. They forfeit not their lands (according to the tenure in Gavel-kind), the Father to Bough, the sonne to Plough."

Matters are vastly different now; a more orderly, upright, and intelligent community than that of North Tyne and Redewater does not exist.

Moss-kennel

On the western acclivity of Busy-gap is a wicket-gate leading to the north. The farm-house of Moss-kennel is to the south of the military road. The site of a mile-castle is next reached; it consists of ground which slopes at the rate of one in five. The Vallum here is good. The accompanying sketch was taken in this vicinity. We

The Knag-burn.

next encounter two narrow, but rather steep gaps, in rapid succession, which do not seem to have obtained names. Advancing a little further, we come to the valley permeated by the Knag-burn, which forms the eastern defence of the famous station of Borcovicus. Before descending into the valley, it will be well to notice the platform on which the station stands—strong on its northern, southern, and eastern sides, and yet comparatively sheltered, and the massive line of Wall which runs up to meet it. The Wall has been brought into its present state by placing the fallen stones on the courses which remained in position. Five courses are original, three replaced.

A Roman villa of considerable size and pretensions once stood on a shelf of the rock, on the east side of the Knag-burn, opposite the middle of the station. It was warmed by hypocausts; and soot was found in the flues. Though removed many years ago, to supply stones for the neighbouring fences, an occasional fragment of tile or tufa marks the spot where it stood. The burn seems to have been dammed back here, so as to furnish a cold bath.

Fortified passage through the Wall.

In the bottom of the valley is a passage through the Wall, which was discovered in 1856; it is thus described by Mr. Clayton: "In the valley of Knag-burn, 371 feet east of the station of Borcovicus, has recently been discovered and explored an unexpected passage through the Roman Wall. It has been closed by double gates, similar to those of the stations; and there is a guard-room on each side. The middle of the gateway guarding the south of the passage is eleven feet three inches. The width of the gateway guarding the north of the passage is ten feet six inches. In the middle there is an upright stone, such as we find in the gateways of the stations, and in the streets of Pompeii. The pathways are on each side of this stone, and the thresholds have been much worn by the feet of the passenger. The two guard chambers are of nearly equal dimensions . . . . During these excavations have been

Ancient remains. found coins of Claudius Gothicus and Constantius, a broken altar, and the usual relics of Roman occupation, fragments of Samian ware and Andernach mill-stones." The object of this gateway has been to give access to a place of entertainment—an amphitheatre on a small scale—which is on the north-side of the Wall. The wood-cut represents it.

Amphitheatre of the garrison.

Its dimensions. It is 100 feet across and about 10 deep. It has no doubt been furnished with wooden seats. The path leading from the gateway to the entrance into the amphitheatre may be traced. Nettles may usually be seen growing in the bottom of it—a sure proof of human presence. Amphitheatres, similar in construction to this, though larger, have been found at Silchester, Dorchester, Banbury, Cirencester, and other places. Even when on a campaign in an enemy's country, amphitheatres were erected for the amusement of the soldiery. Two are represented in the delineations given on Trajan's column at Rome of the Dacian campaigns. Time must often have hung heavily upon the hands of the Tungrian cohort at Borcovicus; what more natural than that they should catch a couple of natives, and set them to slaughter each other for their pleasure! As the pilgrim sits here, and ruminates upon the past and the present of the history of Rome and Britain, he may find food for thought in the following quotation from Dion Cassius:—"Plautius, for having ably managed and concluded the Britannic War, was highly commended by Claudius, and obtained a triumph. And in the gladiatorial combat many freed men, as well as the British captives, fought, numbers of whom he destroyed in this kind of spectacle, and gloried in it."

Britons slaughtered at Rome.

Borcovicus—Housesteads.

The Knag-burn passes the Wall in the way that, probabably, it used to do in Roman times. Between the burn and the station are traces of suburban dwellings; and the old Roman road may be seen winding up to the eastern gateway. The manner in which the Wall unites with the north-east angle of the station should be observed. The station is complete in itself, and was no doubt constructed before the Wall. At the same time no one can doubt that, had not the Wall been placed here, the station of Borcovicus would never have been built. So soon as the Wall was planned, the stations that were to give safe lodgement to its builders and garrisons would be commenced. The Wall, at its junction, has eight courses of stones in position.

Junction of the Wall and Station.

The eastern wall of the station has been cleared of the rubbish which long encumbered it, and is in a good state of preservation. Its masonry differs but little, if at all, from that of the great Wall. It is five feet thick.

We now enter this city of the dead. All is silent; but dead indeed to all human sympathies must the soul of that man be who, in each broken column, each turf-covered mound, each deserted hall, does not recognise a voice telling him, trumpet-tongued, of the rise and fall of empires—of the doom and ultimate destiny of man!

Its position. Housesteads is nearly five miles from the last station, Carrawburgh, and it contains an area of nearly five acres. Its form is the usual one of a parallelogram, rounded at the corners, but its greatest length is from east to west. It is planted on a shelf of basalt, the rock in many places protruding through the superincumbent soil. It slopes gently to the south.

A general survey. If the traveller be not familiar with the usual arrangements of a Roman camp, he had better, before beginning a particular survey, advance to the centre of the station, and make himself acquainted with its plan. One main street, called the *via principalis*, crosses the station from the eastern gate to the western; and another of similar width runs at right angles to it from the northern to the southern gate. The gate nearest the enemy (in this instance the north) was called the Prætorian gate, the one most removed the Decuman. The street leading from the Prætorian gate bore its name. In the case before us, this street is to the east of the central line. Not far from the point where these two main streets intersect each other, the pilgrim will find the solid base of a column, which, if the city had been a mediæval one, would be pronounced to be the pedestal of the market-cross. All the other streets of the station are exceedingly narrow, and lie parallel with the main ones. In this way the whole interior of the camp is divided into parallelograms of greater or less size.

The east gate.

Having taken this general survey, we will now return to the east gate. Like all the other gates of the station, it has been a double one, each portal having folding doors. One of its portals has, at some period before the abandonment of the station by the Romans, been built up. All the other gates have been contracted in a similar manner. This was probably done when the withdrawal of the troops from Britain reduced the mural garrison to a dangerous extent. There are guard-chambers on each side of the gate. On the closing up of the southern section of the gateway, the guard-chamber belonging to it was converted into a dwelling room. When this chamber was excavated in 1833, nearly a cart-load of coals was found in it. The holes in which the pivots of the doors moved will be noticed. The upper part of the door was fixed in a similar manner. This enables us to understand how Samson lifted the gates of Gaza out of their position, and carried them away. The stone against which the gates struck when they were closed remains. We might suppose that this stone would be an obstruction to carriages entering the city. No doubt, however, the kind of chariot used was the *biga*—requiring two horses—and in that case, the horses would allow the stone to pass between them. The horses, too, would probably be small. In the middle of some of the narrow streets of Pompeii, boldly projecting stepping stones occur, which have been placed there for the convenience of foot passengers. These do not seem to have interfered with the transit of wheeled vehicles, as the ruts in the streets show. Here too, as well as at Pompeii, the Roman chariots have left their marks behind them. A rut about eight inches deep appears in the stone threshold of the gateway, on each side of the central stone, evidently caused by the action of wheels. The grooves, which are shewn in the accompanying cut, are a little more than four and a half feet apart.

Ruts in the gateway.

On entering the station, we will keep close to the east wall, and proceed northwards. On the inside of the walls of the station, barracks for the soldiers have no doubt been built, having roofs leaning against the station walls. As, however, these were less carefully constructed than the outside walls, and as they were not "tied" into the main structure, they have, in many instances, disappeared. In this and other stations we have abundant traces of them.

The soldiers' barracks.

Going forward, we see a solid platform of masonry about 20 feet square. Has a catapult been planted here for throwing large stones against the enemy? Lying on the spot is a conical-shaped stone, such as may have been used for such a purpose. Lying near the north wall of the station, which has been increased to nearly twice its original thickness, as if to form a solid bed for a catapult or ballista, are some more of these conical-shaped stones. Stones of similar form have been found in other stations. Their occurrence cannot have been accidental. Probably the superiority of a conical over a spherical missile was known to the Romans. The rudely-formed chamber on the top of this platform is no doubt of late construction In passing the north-east corner, its nicely-rounded form will be noticed. Going forward a little, by the side of the north wall, a mass of ruins is seen, bearing marks of fire. We now pass through the field-gate to examine the outside of the north wall and the north gateway. Excepting the bridge of the North Tyne, this gateway is the finest piece of masonry on the line of the Wall. The large square blocks forming its base have been skilfully and securely laid. Their joints are as close as ever. An inclined roadway led up to this gate, but it was removed at the time of the discovery of the gateway, in order to display its masonry. This gateway, like all the rest at Housesteads, is double. The pillars which, on its outer and inner margin divided it, are both standing. They are of very massive masonry. The east portal of this gateway has been walled up at a comparatively early period. This may be inferred from the fact that, whereas the angles of the stones forming the

Catapult stones.

The north gateway.

basement of the western portal have been much worn by the tread of feet, those of the eastern portal are not injured. The western portal, too, bears marks of change. Its present threshold is about three feet higher than its original one. The station having been devastated by a temporarily triumphant foe (p. 7), has been re-occupied by the Roman troops, without giving themselves time to remove the ruins of their former habitations. Clambering into the portal, its interior arrangements may be viewed. One of the pivot-holes of the gate still retains traces of the oxide of iron—the pivot having probably been shod with iron. The guard-chambers on both sides are in good condition. In the formation of that on the east side a portion of an altar that had been dedicated to Jupiter has been used; the letters I. O. M. *(Jovi optimo maximo)* may still be seen upon it. It will be observed that these chambers have had two floors—an earlier and a later. Before leaving this gate, let the pilgrim once more look at its wide portals and massive masonry, and ask himself if appearances warrant the supposition that the Wall was built when the Roman Empire was in the throes of dissolution, and when the natives of the island, were, as Gildas describes them, "a useless and panic-struck company, equally slow to fight, and ill adapted to run away." Putting out of consideration the strength of the masonry, do these bold apertures indicate any dread of a northern foe? We passed one opening at the Knag-burn, and at the next mile-castle, not a quarter of a mile off, we shall meet with another. Surely the Wall must have been built long before the days of Arcadius, and it can never have been intended as a mere fence to ward off the aggression of the Picts and Scots.

The Wall not a mere fence.

Turning from the gateway to the right, a large stone trough is seen. The stones comprising it are not in their original position. Some of them are grooved, in order to make a tight joint. They are much worn, as if by the sharpening of knives. This trough evidently belongs to a late period of the occupation of the station. It is difficult to conjecture its purpose; has it been used in the preparation of the winter's store of provisions for the garrison? One of the labourers employed in the excavations displayed the unhappy prejudices of a Northumbrian borderer, by giving it as his opinion that the Romans used it for washing their Scotch prisoners in. Near to this was a circular hearth, formed of three courses of Roman tiles. When discovered it was covered with coal-ashes and the scoriæ of iron. It was probably a smithy. The action of the weather and the tread of oxen has nearly destroyed it. The north wall, to the west of this, may next be examined. A second wall, of inferior masonry, has been built inside the first, and the space between them filled up with clay. This gives the wall a considerably increased thickness. It is in this vicinity that some of the stones which may have been intended for the service of the ballista are lying. Proceeding along the wall to the north-west corner of the station, we meet with another chamber, the door of which has been built up.

Stone trough.

Let the student now return to the vicinity of the north gate, and examine the buildings to the south of it. Nearest the gate, and on the west side of the street, extending from the Prætorian to the Decuman gate, is a large apartment, 78 feet long and 18 feet wide. On the south side of

Public buildings.

this is another not quite so long. Its floor is probably supported upon pillars. At the west end of it is a kiln for drying corn, which probably belongs to the moss-trooping times. The steps by which the apartment is reached at the other end are evidently of a late date, and may also be referred to the "troublesome times." This building is strengthened by buttresses. Crossing the Prætorian street, we find a very large building, extending nearly to the east wall, and bounded at its lower margin by the *Via Principalis.* It is 147 feet long and 30 wide. It is strengthened by numerous buttresses. The masonry of it is different from that of the other buildings that we have seen. Its stones are larger, and they have the feathered tooling that we noticed in the facing stones of the abutment of the bridge over the North Tyne. We can scarcely resist the opinion that it belongs to a different period from the other buildings. It may have been one of Severus's restorations. At its eastern extremity are several small rooms: one of them has been heated by underground flues; in another is a cistern or bath, four feet long and three broad, which, when discovered, was coated with cement. Some of these large buildings were no doubt the halls in which the public business of the district was transacted, and others were used as the residences of the præfect and his chief officers.

Soldiers' barracks.

Proceeding once more to the intersection of the main streets, we make our way to the southern gate. We soon come to a considerable mass of building on our right hand. Part of it was excavated in 1858, an enormous mass of debris having been removed. It is not easy to assign a use to each apartment. One of them, when first opened, strongly resembled (though on a small scale) an Italian kitchen; there were marks of fire on its raised hearth. In this part of the camp the ordinary soldiers would dwell. No remains sufficiently perfect exist to give us a complete idea of a Roman house in these military cities. Judging from the remains which do exist, they seem to have been of a dark and gloomy character. No windows have been found; but in most of the stations window-glass is met with in the debris. Probably a frame-work of timber usually intervened between the upper part of the walls of a house and the roof, and here windows were inserted, as well as apertures for the admission of air. Rome, prior to the great fire in Nero's reign, seems to have been built in this manner. We now reach the south gateway. It forms an interesting study. Here all the main features characterizing the other gateways will be recognized. It is of the same massive character; it has a guard-chamber on each side, and the pivot-holes on which the gates rotated are seen. When excavated, the eastern portion of the gateway was found to have been walled up. This must have been done before the houses in front of it were built, the foundations of which are now to be seen. The entrance into the guard-chamber has been closed, and amongst the materials used in doing this, the fragment of a circular shaft will be noticed. But this is not the only instance which we have here of the adaptation of former materials to present purposes. Centuries after the abandonment of the station by the Romans, some mosstrooper seems to have chosen this spot for his habitation. He had little difficulty in converting the guard-chamber and contiguous buildings to his own purposes. The "byer" in which he folded his cattle at night, the kiln

South gate.

Mosstrooper's peel.

Kiln for drying, Grain.

in which he dried his unripened grain, and the lower part of the flight of steps by which he ascended to the little fortress that was his own habitation, may all be distinguished.

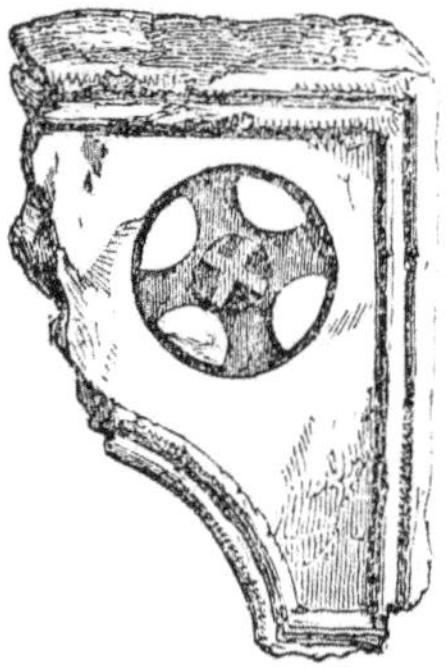

Stone slabs with a circular head-way are often seen lying beside the gates of this and other stations. They have probably formed the top of the door-way leading into the guard-chambers. In the spandril of a fragment of one, at the south gate-way here, is an ornament resembling a Maltese cross.

South Wall of the Station.

The south wall of the station is in a good state of preservation; it stands ten or twelve courses high. The wood-cut

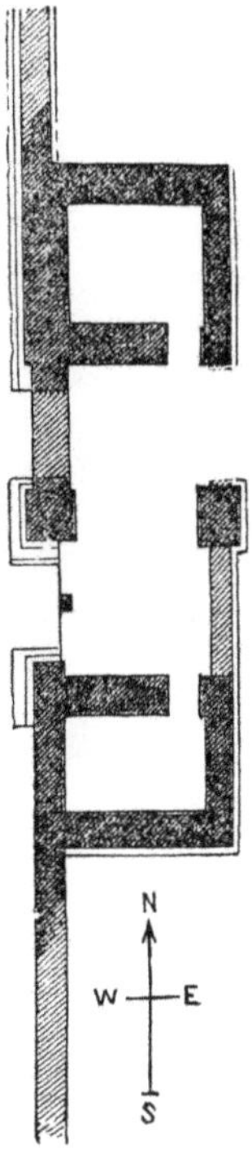

represents it. Its south-west angle deserves examination; it has been repaired in Roman times with stones of a different character from those used in its original construction.

The west gate.

Proceeding along the west wall of the station, we have the opportunity of contemplating a noble piece of Roman masonry, eleven courses high. The west gate — the *Porta Principalis dextra* — is more perfect than any of the rest. The wood-cut in the margin exhibits the plan of it. As usual it has been contracted to half its width; but, to expose an intruding foe to greater difficulty, the passage was rendered diagonal by closing up the northern portion of the outside gate and the southern portion of the inside gate. The inner of these interpolated walls is nearly all removed; the other is nodding to its fall. The wood-cut on the next page shows the gate as seen from the outside. As is uniformly the case in all the gateways, the masonry is strong and massive, the stones being larger and better dressed than those of the other parts of the Wall. The threshold, even of the closed portal, has been worn by the tread of feet. In several places there are indications that the soldiers, whilst loitering about the gate, have employed themselves in sharpening their knives or weapons upon the projecting stones. When the gateway was excavated, the central stone against which the gates struck, was found in the position shewn in the drawing. The guard-chambers are

in an encouraging state of preservation, as the wood-cut, which represents the gate as seen from the inside of the

camp, shows. When these chambers were excavated, they were covered up to the top of the walls with earth, in which was a large quantity of bones and other animal matter. They have been warmed by flues going round the walls. Guard Chambers.

South of the gateway are some buildings intimately connected with the Wall, which were excavated in 1858. At the south-west angle of the station is an ordinary chamber, which, when discovered, was paved with tiles. A walk by the side of the south wall brings us once more to the south gateway.

In wandering over the station, many remnants of Roman occupation will catch the eye. Broken columns may be seen here and there, indicating the love of architecture which existed among the Roman soldiery. Fragments of pottery are very common. The red kind called Samian has never been reproduced since the Roman days. Portions of mortars in which they prepared their food are not uncommon, and occasionally a part of a wine amphora may be picked up. Rough stone troughs are common. Fragments of mill-stones lie about. In all the Roman stations in the North of England, mill-stones, formed of a volcanic stone which has been brought from Andernach on the Rhine, are found. It is hard, porous, and when struck rings like cast metal. Boars' tusks, the horns of deer, and bones of various animals, are tolerably abundant. Coins are scarce. Miscellaneous Remains.

In front of the station are several objects of interest. The farm-house which stood near the south gateway has been removed, and a new one built in a more convenient situation. The well which supplied the house was supposed to be Roman. It is about fifteen feet deep, and is cased with Roman stones, excepting the last yard, which is sunk into the whin rock. The late Mrs. Routeledge told the writer that she used to be a frequent visitor at Housesteads when her grandfather, Mr. William Magnay, resided there, and that *he* sunk the well in front of the house for his own convenience. The pilgrim, if he be from the south country, will by this time have found out that the inhabitants of Northumberland do not affect the tenuosity of speech natural to those born within the sound of Bow Bell, and will be able to appreciate the following circumstance: —Two pilgrims arrived at Housesteads. The weather was unfavourable, and by the time they had completed their survey they were drenched to the skin. Cold and weary, they called at the farm-house for information as to their sleeping quarters. Before leaving, they were asked if they would like a glass of ***Roman water***. One of the shivering antiquaries thinking that a little ***Rum and water*** in present circumstances might be highly beneficial, gratefully accepted of the offer. What was his horror to see the hind take a bucket, and repair to the supposed Roman well! To the credit of the strangers, they both quaffed the cooling fluid with a good grace, and pronounced it excellent. (*Tour along the Roman Wall*, by James Wardell.)

The Northern Doric.

Suupplies of Water.

The Tungrian cohort, had however, no lack of water. There is a spring to the north of the crags which they seem to have enclosed with masonry; the remains of a well have been found near the spot where the Knag-burn passes under the Wall, and there is a very abundant spring of excellent water at the bottom of the slope in front of the station.

The whole of the bank in front of the station is covered with the foundations of streets and houses. To the west of these are long terraced lines, which have no doubt been devoted to cultivation, after a mode still practised in Italy and other continental countries. The plain below, which has recently been drained, seems to have been the burial-ground of the station. In cutting the drains, numerous human remains were found. Two stones that have formed portions of circular columns of great magnitude are lying in this valley. They have probably rolled down from the station above. A ridge, caused by the protuberance of the sandstone rock, rises gently out of the plain at our feet. It is called Chapel Hill. Some considerable temple is supposed to have stood upon it. Many altars have been found here. One of them is represented in the wood-cut. It may be translated —"To Jupiter, the greatest and best, and the deities of Augustus, the first cohort of Tungrians (a miliary one), commanded by Quintus Verius Superstis Præfect [erected this]". To the west of Chapel Hill is the site of the semi-subterranean cave, dedicated to the worship of Mithras, which

Terraced Cultivation.

Chapel Hill.

Mithraic Cave.

was discovered in 1822. It is described with considerable minuteness by Mr. Hodgson, in the *Arch. Æl.*, O.S., v. i., p. 263, &c. The worship of Mithras — the Sun, or the Persian Apollo—was introduced from the East into Europe about the time of Julius Cæsar. The mysteries connected with it were supposed to have involved the sacrifice of human victims and various other abominations. Edicts were issued for its suppression by Hadrian and others, but in vain.

Amongst the altars found in the cave here, was one bearing the names of Gallus and Volusianus, who were consuls in the year 253. There was also found the tablet here engraved, which represents Mithras himself, surrounded by an egg-shaped belt, containing the signs of the Zodiac. The site of the temple is now nearly obliterated. There can be little doubt that when the mythology of Greece and Rome had lost hold of the sympathies of the community, the worship of Mithras was pressed upon the attention of mankind, in opposition to the verities of Christianity.

The antiquities found at Housesteads have been so numerous and so important, that any attempt to recapitulate them here would be perfectly vain. Two or three may be

selected as a specimen of the rest. The mutilated figure here represented was recently found near the east gate-

Figures of Victory.

way of the station. Victory must have been a favourite goddess with the Tungrians. Several statues of her have been found here. She is usually represented careering with outstretched wings over a subject world; she carries a palm branch in her left hand, a laurel crown in her right. The

Deæ Matres.

worship of the Deæ Matres — the good mothers — whose name it was not lucky to mention, was much in vogue with the Gothic portion of the Roman community. Several statues of them have been found here; two of which are shown

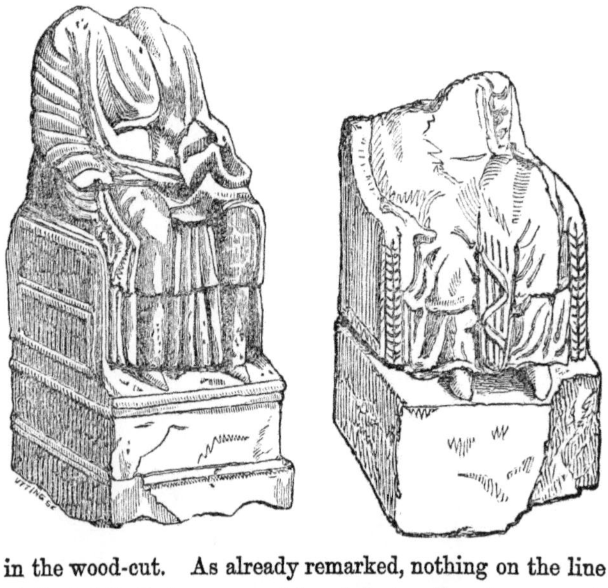

in the wood-cut. As already remarked, nothing on the line of the Wall that was capable of destruction has escaped the effects of Caledonian vengeance, and all these sculptures show it. Only one more allusion to the antiquities

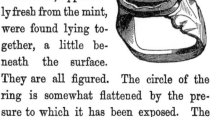

of this station can be indulged in. In a paper read by Mr. Clayton before the Society of Antiquaries of Newcastle, in 1853, the following facts appeared. In clearing the ground in front of the south gateway of the station, a gold signet ring, a gold pendant for the ear, and a coin of Commodus, apparently fresh from the mint, were found lying together, a little beneath the surface. They are all figured. The circle of the ring is somewhat flattened by the presure to which it has been exposed. The coin dates from the third consulship of Commodus, corresponding with the year of Christ, 181. It was about this period that the terrible

Gold Relics.

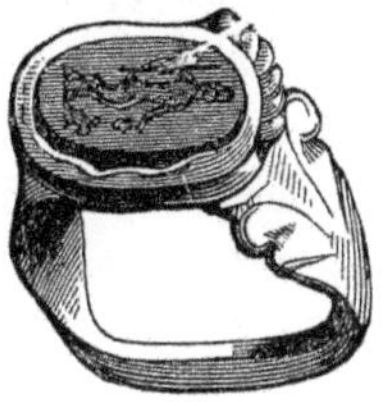

disasters, recorded by Dion Cassius, and which are referred to in the introductory chapter of this work, (p. 7.) took place.

Their historical value. The inference is not improbable, that these ornaments were worn by some Roman chieftain and his lady, who were slain when making their escape from the south gate of the city at the time of the general devastation.

Mr. McLauchlan has laid down a Roman road, extending from Housesteads, in a south-easterly direction, to the "Stanegate" or "Causeway" at Grindon Hill (*Mem.*, p. 40.) The writer had no difficulty in tracing it as Mr. McLauchlan has described it, from the vicinity of the Moss-kennel farm-house to Grindon-shield. Horsley was of opinion that another branch road went in a south-westerly direction to join the "Stanegate" near Chesterholm. The writer has sometimes thought that he saw traces of this road, particularly at a place south of the present turnpike road, opposite the 30th mile-stone. After considerable examination, however, Mr. McLauchlan could not satisfy himself as to its existence, and therefore does not insert it.

Branch Roads.

No one who carefully examines the station of Borcovicus can help admiring the skill and care with which the excavations have been conducted. Whilst expressing our great obligations to the presiding genius of the whole, its learned and patriotic proprietor, it is but justice to name two humble labourers.—Walter Rutherford (unhappily now no more) and Anthony Place, who still wields the pick-axe and spade, to whose zeal and intelligence the antiquary is much indebted.

North-west angle. On leaving the station, it will be well to notice the junction of the Wall with the north-west angle of the station. Here, as we saw was the case on the eastern side, the station is independent of the Wall. Some repairs have been made in this corner, and longitudinal stones with the feathered "broaching" introduced. The subjoined wood-cut

represents it. The remains of suburban buildings will be observed outside the west gate of the station.

We now proceed on our journey westward. Those to whom it is an object to avoid fatigue will best consult their ease by proceeding along the Roman military-way, which will be easily found. All the field-gates are placed upon it. The gentle pilgrim does not need to be reminded how needful it is in a pastoral country to close the gates after him. This military-way was in actual use not very long ago. The family of Wright were hereditary carriers between Newcastle and Carlisle for more than 100 years, and so continued till driven off the road by the rail. The present representative of the family is tenant of the Housesteads farm. The tradition in the family is, that the traffic was originally conducted on pack-horses, and that the carriers, in the central

The Roman Military-way.

part of their journey between Newcastle and Carlisle, were accustomed to resort to the Roman road. They occasionally camped out all night, and one of their camping places was opposite "Twice-brewed Ale," a carriers' inn contemporaneous with the turnpike road.

The walk along the cliffs is exceedingly beautiful, and the Wall for the most part is in excellent condition, all the way to Hot-bank. The traveller will notice, too, that it differs in width in different places, as is shown by the offsets and insets which occasionally occur. No doubt different gangs of workmen wrought simultaneously on different parts of the line, and the superintendent of each was allowed to exercise, within certain limits, his own judgment as to the width of the Wall. On the north face of the Wall the line is continuous. At the distance of two furlongs from Housesteads, and seven from the last that we noticed, above Mosskennel, is another mile-castle. It is plain from this and other examples, that the position of the mile-castles was not influenced by the contiguity of a station. At the time of the publication of the second edition of *The Roman Wall*, this mile-castle was covered with turf. It was thus spoken of:—"Its ruins are sufficiently conspicuous to invite the use of the pickaxe and spade." This attention it has now received, by Mr. Clayton's direction, and it forms an interesting object of study. The castle has adapted itself to the rocky site on which it has been placed, and which is very uneven—dipping chiefly to the north. The great Wall forms the north wall of the castle, and stands 14 courses or 9½ feet high. This is the finest specimen remaining on the whole line. The castle itself measures, on the inside,

The Wall differs in width in different places.

The Housesteads Mile-castle.

The castle described.

57 feet 7 inches from west to east, and 49 feet 7 inches from north to south. The thickness of the east and west walls of the castle is 9 feet. The thickness of the Wall at the north gateway—and it always assumes additional width at the gateways—is not less than 10 feet. The southern angles of the castle are rounded exteriorly, but are square in the inside. It will be noticed, that in building the walls of the castle, occasional courses of sandstone slate have been used for bonding, very much in the way that tiles are, in the Roman structures of southern Britain. An inspection of the south-east corner will shew that this angle has been built before the contiguous parts, and that it formed a sort of buttress for the adjacent walls to lean upon. The same arrangement will be noticed on both sides of the jambs of the north gateway. The north gateway may now attract our attention. It is obviously of two periods. The original portal is of most substantial masonry, and has an opening ten feet wide. It has been spanned by an arch. The springers of the arch are in position, and several of the arch-stones lie upon the ground. Each stone has a luis-hole in it, which is so placed as to facilitate the bringing of the inner edge of the stone into its proper place in the arch. The height of the gate, from the floor to the impost of the arch, is a little under six feet. At some period subsequent to its original structure, the width of this gateway has been reduced to 3 feet 9 inches. The floor of this new gateway is 3½ feet above the sill of the original. In order to understand these arrangements, we must now revert to the facts which were revealed at the time of the excavation. On digging down to the foundations of the castellum, on the

Bonding stones instead of tiles.

The luis made use of.

inside of the north wall, a number of masons' chippings were met with, and a mason's chisel. Upon the chippings, in the neighbourhood of the walls, had been laid a flooring of rough flags. These flags, however, were much broken, and some of the fragments were forced into an almost vertical position, all indicating that the walls of the building had been forcibly thrown down. Immediately above the flags was found a quantity of finely comminuted charcoal, as if the sheds or barrack-rooms, which probably were placed against the main walls of the building, had been destroyed by fire. The ashes were not found in the centre of the area. At this level were discovered an axe and a knife, resembling those carved on altars. The destruction here indicated, doubtless, took place in the reign of Commodus. Above the mass of stones, mortar, and rubbish, a second floor and a second series of buildings connected with the main walls were found. In order to shew the height of the second floor, the part immediately in front of the north gateway has been left unexcavated. The south gateway is in a ruinous state, but it has evidently been diminished in width as well as the other. The masonry of the repairs is quite Roman in its character. In conducting the excavations, numerous fragments of Samian ware were found. A fragment of a vase had the word *dedico* scratched upon it. Some roofing-tiles and slates were found, as well as some coins of Hadrian and Antoninus Pius. The most valuable relic, however, was a portion of a slab containing a record of the second legion, and of Hadrian's legate, Aulus Platorius Nepos. When complete, it was no doubt the same as those found in the next two

The guard-rooms placed against the walls—the centre vacant.

A Hadrian slab.

castella. This stone had formed part of the flooring of the renovated structure; it is much worn. To complete the history of this castellum, it may be stated that, above this second floor, another layer of wood ashes was found, redder in colour and smaller in quantity than the former, and that a mass of broken stones and earth covered up the whole. It would seem as if a second time the enemy had used his devastating force, and that the building had never again been restored. On the inside of the east wall of the castellum, near the south-east angle, is a small recess, which, when first opened, was black with soot and charcoal-dust. It has no doubt been a fire-place, but it has no chimney.

A second overthrow.

The hill ascending from the opening we meet with on the west side of this mile-castle is called Cuddy's-crag. The next opening is called the Rapishaw-gap. The view here introduced is from the western side of this gap, looking eastward.

Rapishaw-gap.

Our course now lies over a considerable eminence, which leads us down to Hot-bank. The view from the summit is very extensive and fine. All the four lakes—Broomlee, Greenlee, Crag Lake, and Grindon, are in sight. Not far from the western margin of Greenlee, is Bonnyrig, a shooting-box belonging to Sir Edward Blackett. The course of the crags to the east and west of us will be viewed with interest. Beyond the waste to the north-east are the Simonside Hills, and beyond them is the Cheviot range. The heather-clad hill immediately to the south of us is Borcum, now called

Barcombe hill.

Barcombe, from which the Romans procured much of their stone, and from which the name of the station of *Borcovicus* is no doubt derived. The defile leading by its western flank to the Tyne will be noticed, and the propriety of guarding it by a stationary camp perceived. The platform of the station of Vindolana may be distinguished by its peculiarly verdant surface. On the south side of the Tyne, Langley Castle may be noticed—near the angle of a large plantation; beyond it are the chimneys of the smelt-mills. The valley of the river Allan is seen joining that of the Tyne; and near the confluence of the two rivers, may be discerned the ruins of Staward Peel. In the distance, to the south-west of us,

The Cumberland mountains.

are the lofty summits of Cross-fell, Skiddaw, and Saddleback.

The farm-house of Bradley stands on the tail of the crag on which we now are. Built up in the doorway of the old kitchen, was one-half of the Hadrian slab, which will presently be noticed. On the other side of the modern military-

Bradley Hall.

road stood a farm-house, dignified by the name of Bradley Hall. It was once a place of importance, and even now the foundations of considerable buildings may be traced. It appears that Edward I. resided at it, in Sept. 1306, on his last journey to Scotland. (*Arch. Inst. Journal,* vol. xiv., p. 268.)

Passing onward, Crag Lake comes fully into view. We

now descend into the valley of the Milking-gap. There are distinct traces of a mile-castle in the defile. In its Milking-gap.

ruins were found the inscribed stone shown here; the

left hand portion of which is now at Durham, the right (which came from Bradley) at Matfen. The farm-house of Hot-bank is a sunny spot in the memory of many pilgrims —not a few having here received much kind attention.

Vindolana—Chesterholm.

We may now forsake the Wall for a little, in order to pay a visit to the station of VINDOLANA, the modern Chesterholm; it is about a mile due south from Hot-bank. A bridle-road by the side of the burn running out of Crag Lake takes us down to the military-road. Before crossing the Vallum, some circles and other enclosures, formed of whin-stones, are seen on the right hand. They are probably of ancient British construction. The Vallum makes two rapid curves in this neighbourhood, assuming something like the form of the letter S, apparently to avoid the contiguous marsh; this is best seen from the heights. Crossing the turnpike-road, we pass two cottages, called

High Shields

High Shields, and then descend into the valley. It is not improbable that the road we tread upon is the remains of a Roman one. Before coming to the station, a large

Barrow.

barrow—possibly the burial-place of some British chief—may be noticed. On the south side of it is a Roman mile-

Roman mile-stone.

stone, the only one in Britain standing in its original position. This mile-stone stands upon a line of road which extended from CILURNUM to MAGNA, and probably further in both directions. The position of both of these stations, and that also of VINDOLANA, warrant the supposition that they were planted by Agricola. The road which connected them would not be altogether disused after the Wall was built.

Another mile-stone stood, some years ago, to the west of this, but it was broken up for a gate-post. This, Horsley tells us, had on it the remarkable inscription, in large coarse letters, BONO REIPVBLICAE NATO, which was intended as a compliment to the emperor then reigning. The farm-house near the mile-stone is called Coadley-gate. Coadley-gate

The station stands advantageously. Though it occupies an elevated platform, it is sheltered by an amphitheatre of hills, and is naturally protected on every side but the west. The walls, ditches, and gateways, though in a dilapidated condition, may be easily made out. It has an area of 3¼ acres. To the west of the station are the ruins of an extensive building, which has been furnished with hypocausts. The pillars long retained the marks of fire and soot, which gave rise to the popular belief that a colony of fairies had here established themselves, and that this was their kitchen. To the west of this ruin is a series of gutter-stones (some of which have been laid bare), by means of which water has been brought from a neighbouring spring. The ornamental cottage in the valley was built by the late Rev. Anthony Hedley, an earnest and able antiquary. With the exception of the quoins and lintels, it is constructed of stones chiseled only by Roman hands. Some valuable antiquities have, at various times, been discovered here, chiefly by Mr. Hedley. As the wayfarer may wish for a memorial of them, drawings of a few are introduced. The finest is the large altar shewn on the succeeding page. It has been translated:—"To Jupiter, the best and greatest, and to the rest of the immortal gods, and to the genius of the Prætorium; Quintus Petronius Urbicus, son of Quintus,

Vindolana described.

Large altar to Jupiter.

and of the Fabian tribe, præfect of the fourth cohort of the Gauls, from Italy, a native of Brixia, performed a vow for himself and family." This station was garrisoned by

the fourth cohort of Gauls. In the walls of the covered passage leading from the kitchen of the cottage to the burn side, several Roman stones have been built up. Amongst them is one in which the pivot of one of the gates has been inserted; several coping-stones; a fragment of an inscription to Hadrian, similar to that which so frequently occurs in the mile-castles; a stone recording the name of the 20th legion, which was styled the Valerian and the Victorious, and whose badge was a boar; with several others. In the front wall of the house is a triangular stone, on which are carved a cockatrice, a globe, a crescent, a cross, and, at the top, a small circular knob, which Hodgson terms "The umbilicated moon." The sculpture is supposed to have reference to the mysteries of Mithraic worship. It was found in the farm-house of Low Foggerish. Other antiquities.

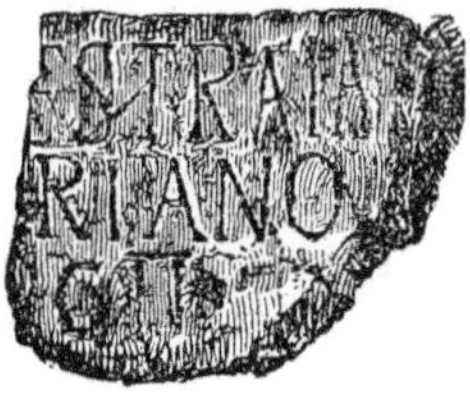

The stream which flows out of Crag Lake is joined near the mile-stone by another from Winshields, when the united rivulet takes the name of the Chineley Burn. A little further down, just below a rustic bridge, water is seen bubbling up in the middle of the stream. This is caused by the surplus water of Grindon Lough, which, having flowed The Chineley Burn.

for two miles and a half underground, finds vent at this place.

Barcombe Hill.

Should the traveller have time, and the day be clear, he will do well to ascend the hill of Barcombe. From the top, an excellent view is obtained of the line of mural fortification. Some of the Roman quarries will be noticed. In one of them, near "the Long-stone," a small copper vessel was found in 1835, carefully deposited beneath the stone-chippings. It contained sixty-three coins, which seem to have been wrapped up in a piece of leather; part of which remained. Three of the coins are of gold; the rest are silver denarii. The gold coins belong to the reigns of Claudius, Nero, and Vespasian. Of the silver coins, nine are consular; the rest are imperial, extending from the time of Nero to that of Hadrian. No less than seventeen of them are coins of Trajan; four belong to the time of Hadrian. As the coins of Trajan are more numerous than those of any other, and as his coins and those of Hadrian are in excellent preservation, the conclusion is natural that this deposit of coins was made in Hadrian's reign. This inference strongly favours the idea that Hadrian did not content himself with casting up an earthen mound, but that he wrought quarries and built the Wall. In order to show the excellent preservation of the coins of Hadrian, accurate drawings of two of them are here introduced.

The Thorngrafton find.

This hill-top has another object of interest for the antiquary. A little to the east of the Long-stone, and on a platform which, though it is a little below the summit, commands a view of the mural ridge from Sewingshields to the Nine Nicks of Thirlwall, is an ancient camp, of the kind usually ascribed to the aboriginal Britons. Besides the principal intrenchment, which is of an irregular oval shape, there are other lines of defence on the eastern side, which is naturally the weakest. An inner fortification near the west end of the principal inclosure has a ditch and rampart of its own. A sort of covered way, passing into a series of circular cavities, runs along the edge of the cliff facing the Wall. From these hiding-places the occupants have no doubt often watched their enemy. Ancient British Camp.

Should the pilgrim, at this stage of his journey, betake himself to Bardon Mill—distant a little more that a mile—for rest, refreshment, or the rail, he should not fail to notice, and, if possible, to visit, the ancient mediæval stronghold of Willimontswick, on the south side of the Tyne. It consists of a square inclosure, which has no doubt had a tower at each angle. The entrance-tower still remains. The cattle were driven into the inclosure at night, or stalled in the byers communicating with it; while the farm-servants occupied the upper story of the barracks, which they entered by flights of stone steps. Mediæval digression. Willimontswick Castle.

Willimontswick Castle has a special interest to most Englishmen, as having been the birthplace of Nicholas Ridley, Bishop of London. He was burnt at Oxford, with Hugh Latimer, Bishop of Worcester, on the 16th of October, 1555. The letters of this noble-minded Northumbrian, written in Bishop Ridley.

the immediate prospect of his death, have a peculiar charm to the dwellers upon the South Tyne, independently of their elevated tone and scholarly English. He refers to the customs of the Border country, and to his relatives in many well-known localities of the district. Unhappily, the narrow limits of this little book prohibit extracts. The accompanying wood-cut gives a general view of Willimontswick Castle.

The Cliffs. Returning to Hot-bank, we now resume our companionship with the Wall. The cliffs along which we walk, and the lake below, are interesting objects of contemplation. A number of goats, in a half-wild state, used to frequent these crags, adding to their romantic aspect; but they have recently disappeared. Not long ago one unhappy goat (before the destruction of the flock) got perched upon a needle of basalt, midway in the cliff. Here he remained nine days, and then leapt from the cliff; but was eventually found dead, having, it is supposed, drunk too freely of the water of the lake.

The next gap is in the grounds belonging to the Steel-rig farm. The Steel-gri-gap. Here the Wall may be studied to great advantage. Owing to the rapid dip of the hill, the stones are laid parallel to the horizon. The mode of forming the interior of the Wall will be noticed. After disposing of a course of rubble-stones, in a slanting position, a layer of mortar has been laid upon the top of them, and then another course of stones. The wood-cut shews the present aspect of the Wall at this point, as viewed from the

north. The Wall again ascends a hill to the west of the Steel-rig-gap, and after turning sharply to the north, almost immediately descends again into the gap called the Castle-nick. This name is no doubt derived from the cas- The Castle-nick.

tellum here, and which was, in 1854, freed from its encumbering rubbish by Mr. Clayton. The wood-cut shews its present appearance, as viewed from the west. Crag Lake

and Hot-bank are seen in the distance. The walls of this mile-castle, which are seven feet thick, are in excellent preservation, having six or seven courses of stone standing. The castle measures 50 feet from east to west, and 62 from north to south, inside measurement. The gateways do not present the usual massive masonry; they have doubtless been altered since their original construction. The rubbish which encumbered the site impressed the excavators with the idea that the walls of the building had been purposely thrown down. The chief peculiarity about this castle is, that the foundations of the interior apartments of the building still remain, on its western side. These erections have been quite independent of the main walls of the castle, and have been more rudely constructed. In front of this mile-castle are traces of some works which may belong to the ancient British period. Here, too, the structure of the Roman military-way may be studied to advantage. The important inscription which is here given was, there is reason to believe, derived from this castle. It was long in the pos-

Hadrian inscription.

J STOREY DEL. SB. UTTING. SC

session of Mr. Lowes, of Ridley Hall, but is now in the museum of the Society of Antiquaries of Newcastle. (See the Society's *Catalogue*, p. 26.)

Cats' Stairs.

A little further on, another depression in the mural ridge, called the Cats' Stairs, is reached. The view given on the next page is taken from the north side of it. Should the pilgrim wish to have a view of the crags along which the Wall runs, he would do well to go down the Cats' Stairs, and walk along the plain to the north of the Wall as far as the next gap, which is the great defile at Peel-crag. After passing the first elevation west of the Cats' Stairs, we come to the opening west of the Peel-crag.

Peel-crag.

As the defile at Peel-crag is wider than usual, special precautions have been taken to defend it. On both sides of the pass the Wall bends sharply to the south: this has the double effect of narrowing the gorge, and exposing an enemy to a flanking-fire within half a bow-shot on both sides. It is not unlikely that the low ground north of the Wall was

CATS' STAIRS, p. 153.

a swamp in the days of the Romans. The road which passes through the defile leads to Keilder, and so into Scotland; in its progress northwards it soon degenerates into a mere track. To the south of the Wall, by the side of the military-way, is a house, once well known as the "Twice-brewed" inn. As many as twenty men and forty horses used to be put up here on a carriers' night. It is now a lonely farm-house.

'Twice-brewed' Inn.

On the western side of Peel-crag, sheltered by a few trees, is the now-deserted farm-house of Steel-rig. Here the Wall loses the basaltic ridge, and runs along a stratum of sandstone. The Wall is in bad condition, but the fosse, with a rampart on its outer margin, is boldly developed. The crags shortly re-appear, and the ditch again ceases. Before reaching the top of Winshields—just where the fosse ceases—a mile-castle is met with; it is about eight furlongs from that at Castle-nick. Winshields is about 1000 feet above the sea. The prospect from it is very extensive in every direction. On a clear day the vessels navigating the Solway can easily be descried. Burnswark and Criffell, well-known heights in Dumfriesshire, come into view.

Steel-rig.

Winshields.

Proceeding onwards from this point, we find the Wall in an encouraging state of preservation. A little friendly help has been used to make the facing-stones on each side equal the height of the core of the interior. "At about a furlong west of the top of Winshields, and about 80 yards south of the Wall, is a sheltered spot, called Green Slack, in which are some foundations, apparently sites of ancient [British] residences; thence crossing a deep valley, called Lodham Slack, where the Wall requires its ditch again, we gain a summit, where are traces of [ancient British] encampments, close to the Wall." (*McLauchlan's Memoir*, p. 44.) A gentle descent now brings us to Shield-on-the-Wall—a thatched cottage, which is about to be removed. It probably stands upon the site of a mile-castle, and is composed of its materials. Haltwhistle is about three miles distant from this point.

Green Slack.

Lodham Slack.

Ancient British encampments.

Shield-on-the-Wall.

Nearly due south from Shield-on-the-Wall, is a large stone lying on the edge of the south agger of the Vallum, which Mr. McLauchlan thinks "has the appearance of having been a cromlech, one of the supporters being still under it in a broken state." (*Mem.*, p. 44.)

Bogle-hole. We next come to a gap of bold proportions, having the ominous name of Bogle-hole. Caw-gap. The next gap is Caw-gap. A cattle-shed, formed out of a ruined cottage, stands in it. The extreme jealousy with which the Romans defended an exposed situation is well shown here; the fosse which guards the pass through the low ground is discontinued on the western side as soon as the crag attains a sufficient elevation, but upon the ground's drooping, though only for the space of a few yards, it re-appears for that short distance. A road passes through this gap, north and south. Northwards is a solitary house, called Burn-Deviot, long the resort of smugglers and sheep-stealers. Lights, as the shepherds believe, are still to be seen at night flickering about the windows—the spirits of those who have been murdered in it. After passing Caw-gap, the Wall is for some distance nearly uprooted. To the south of us two large stones are seen standing. They are called "The Mare and Foal." In Armstrong's Map of Northumberland three are marked. They are probably remains of a Druidical circle. Proceeding onwards, we come to a part of the Wall where it diminishes in thickness one foot at a single step. The cliffs once more begin to assume a columnar form; the Vallum is well developed. Passing Bloody-gap, and another gap called Thorny-Doors, we find the Wall once more in an excellent state of preservation, and it continues so for a considerable distance. Cawfields. The farm-house to the north is called Cawfields. In the next gap, named by the peripatetic party of 1849 the Pilgrims'-gap, is a mile-castle of great interest. It was excavated by Mr. Clayton in 1848. It measures 63 feet from east to west, and 49 from north to south, inside measurement. Its walls have seven or eight courses of stone standing, and they are eight feet thick. The massive masonry of both northern and southern gates may be studied to advantage. They have an opening ten feet wide. The pivot-holes of the gates remain. At each side of the entrance here is a recess in the wall for receiving the gate when thrown back.

Inscriptions found in it.

Two inscribed stones were found in this castle. One of them is an old monumental stone, which has evidently been converted into a hearth-stone. The inscription has been thus expanded :—*Diis Manibus. Dagvaldus miles Pannoniæ vixit annos . . Pusinna* [*sua*] *conjux titulum* [*posuit.*] "To the divine shades—Pusinna erected this tablet to the memory of her husband, Dagvaldus, a soldier of Pannonia." The other inscribed stone was still more fragmentary, but a comparison of the drawing of it here given, with those of the

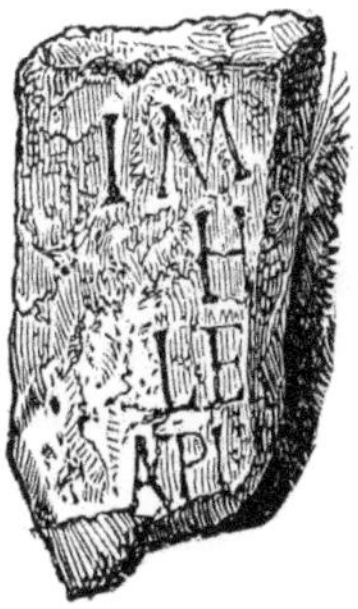

more perfect inscriptions found in the Milking-gap and the Castle-nick castles, will show its meaning and value. This castellum is $7\frac{3}{4}$ furlongs from the last one at Shield-on-the-Wall. "Hence it would seem," says Mr. McLauchlan, "that the distances between the four last castles are the greatest on the line."

We turn our steps 'in by.'

A road leads from the vicinity of the mile-castle to the town of Haltwhistle, in the sheltered valley of the South Tyne, whither, should the shades of evening be approaching, the way-worn antiquary may be glad to bend his steps.

Haltwhistle, and the way to it.

Just before reaching General Wade's military-road, a Roman camp will be observed. On the sides which are most exposed, double and triple lines of earth-works have been raised. It is on the line of the Roman road leading from Cilurnum to Magna. It has no doubt been occupied during the construction of the Wall. A quarry by the burn-side was used by the Romans. Mr. Clayton, in 1847, discovered on the face of it the letters

An earthen intrenchment.

LEG. VI. V.

Legio Sexta Victrix; but the inscription was soon afterwards wilfully obliterated. Haltwhistle is about a mile and a half from this point.

The Castle-hill.

At Haltwhistle there are at least three objects of interest— the Castle-hill, the church, and the old manor-house. The Castle-hill is a natural mound of earth, but has at some early period been fortified. Earthen ramparts encompass it on every side except the south. The old Scotch firs which grow upon it give it a picturesque appearance. At the east end of the town near the Castle-hill is a fine old peel, said to be the ancient manor-house. There was formerly another strong peel on the west side of the bridge to defend the entrance into the town. The church is of the early English style of architecture; it has three elegant lancet windows at its east end, and trefoiled sedilia. On the left of the altar lies a recumbent figure; its legs are gone, but it still displays the well-known corn-sheaves and fess of the Blenkinsops on the shield. On the rights is the remarkable

The Church.

tombstone, figured (under the 14th century) in *Boutell's Christian Monuments.* Partly behind a pew on the left is another stone possessing some interest, as marking by some uncouth rhymes the resting-place of Bishop Ridley's brother, "The Laird of Waltoun." The pews of the 17th century have had their terminations sawn off, and the church generally has suffered not a little. Many of the houses in Haltwhistle have been peel-houses. Supposing the antiquary to have reached Haltwhistle on the previous evening by the public road, let him, on his return to the Wall, vary his route. A footpath will lead him by the side of the Haltwhistle-burn back to the military-road. Here "among rocks gleaming out amid the green trees which shadow them, may be seen the stream, coloured by the moss whence it has come, and brawling over the stony channel till its waves are whitened into foam."

The Town.

Return to the Wall.

Rejoining the Wall where we left it—at the Cawfields mile-castle—we resume our mural investigations. Haltwhistle-burn-head is the first object of interest that we meet with. The burn is derived from the overflowings of Greenlee Lough. Between its source and the Wall it is called Caw-burn; below that point it bears the name of Haltwhistle-burn. Occasionally the stream is too much swollen to admit of the passage of pedestrians; in this case the bridge on the military-road must be resorted to.

Haltwhistle-burn.

Westward of the Burn-head farm-house the fosse is boldly developed, but the Wall is traceable only in the ruins of its foundations. "About mid-way between the water and the station of Æsica are traces of a building about the size of the mile-castles, but, unlike them, being partly within and partly without the Wall. Its distance from the last is only about four furlongs." (*McL.'s Memoir*, p. 44.) Hence it remains a question whether it be a mile-castle or not. Under any circumstances, it is in bad condition.

Æsica—Great Chesters.

The Station described.

ÆSICA, or Great Chesters, is the tenth stationary camp on the line of the Wall. It incloses an area of about three acres. The second cohort of the Astures was stationed

here. The stamp on this fragment of roofing-tile, as well as some lapidary inscriptions, confirm the *Notitia* in this respect. In Gordon's day some of the walls of the station were standing twelve or thirteen feet high; at present all that can be said is, that the ramparts and fosse are clearly defined. Two or more ramparts of earth seem to have given additional security to the western side, which is naturally the weakest. The southern gateway may be traced; it is nearer the eastern than the western side. The western gateway seems to have been walled up before the abandonment of the station. In the centre of the camp is a vaulted

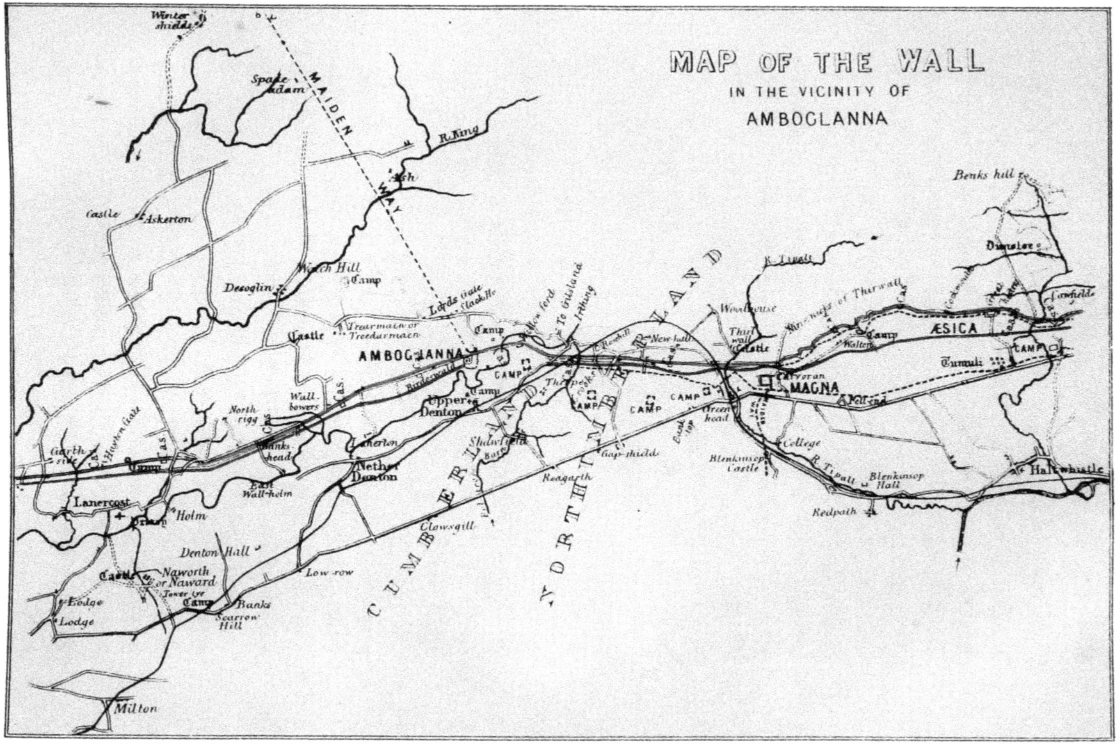
MAP OF THE WALL
IN THE VICINITY OF
AMBOGLANNA
MAIDEN WAY
CUMBERLAND
NORTHUMBERLAND
AMBOGLANNA
MAGNA
ÆSICA
Spade Adam
Winter shields
R. King
Ash
Castle
Askerton
Desoglin
Watch Hill
Camp
Lords Gate
Castle
Trearmain or Treedarmaen
Wall bowers
North rigg
Banks head
Garth side
Hayton Gate
Lanercost
Holm
East Wall-helm
Nether Denton
Upper Denton
Birdoswald
Denton Hall
Naworth or Naward
Lodge
Camp
Banks
Scarrow Hill
Low row
Clowsgill
Milton
To Gilsland
Irthing
Shawfield
Reagarth
Gap-shields
Green head
Blenkinsop Castle
Blenkinsop Hall
College
R. Tipalt
Redpath
Woodhouse
Thirl wall Castle
Nine nicks of Thirwall
Walltown
Carvoran
Tumuli
Benks hill
Dunsloe
Cawfields
Haltwhistle

chamber, which reminds us of a somewhat similar structure in Cilurnum. It has a ledge, perhaps intended for a seat, on the further side. To the south and east of the station are traces of suburban buildings. At some distance down the hill are the remains of a hypocaust. An ancient road leads from the southern gateway of the station to the "Stanegate." In the flat ground south of the station, and in the near neighbourhood of the Vallum, are traces of some barrows and some circular and quadrilateral enclosures. In this vicinity stood Walltown Mill, where the burying-ground of the station seems to have been. Brand observed several remarkable barrows, and was shewn some of the graves which had been opened.

Walltown Mill.

The peculiar feature of this station is the water-course, which is to be found to the north of it. Dr. Lingard knew of it; in his MS. notes he says, "The water for the station was brought by a winding aqueduct, still visible, from the head of Haltwhistle-burn; it winds five miles." But from Dr. Lingard's time to the publication of *The Roman Wall*, it seems to have been lost sight of. The water-course consists of a channel three or four feet deep, and proportionately wide, cut in the sides of the numerous little hills which stud the plain north of the Wall. In order to preserve the water-level, a most circuitous course is taken, but so effectually is this done, that only once has it been necessary to resort to a bridge or embankment. This bridge is now gone, but the place has the name of Benks Bridge. The whole length of the aqueduct is six miles; the distance in a straight line is little more than two miles and a quarter. By this means the water of the Caw-burn was brought

The Water-course.

within a short distance of the station. Within about 350 yards of the station the aqueduct is lost sight of. Owing to the nature of the level, the water could only be brought over this part of its course by means of an artificial embankment; this, if ever it existed, is now entirely removed. It may surprise the reader to find the means of supplying so important an element as water placed on the north of the Wall. The truth is, that the Romans by no means gave up the district beyond the Wall to the enemy. An aqueduct within sight of Æsica was perfectly safe when the forces of Rome were vigorously handled. Should the pilgrim wish personally to trace the water-course, he will get all needful directions from the tenant of Great Chesters, Mr. Edward Lowes, from whom the writer derived, in the first instance, his information.

Shortly after leaving Æsica, the crags again appear, and the Wall ascends the heights. For some distance little more than the foundation-courses remain in position. The fosse, which at first is distinct, is soon discontinued. Soon after passing Cockmount Hill farm-house, we meet with a long and very encouraging tract of the Wall. Its north face exhibits six and seven courses of facing-stones, and in some places as many as nine; the south face is broken. Before coming to Ollalee farm-house, the ruins of a mile-castle, very distinctly marked, are met with, at the distance of $7\frac{1}{4}$ furlongs from Æsica. Opposite the farm-house the Wall is reduced to a pitiable condition, and it continues so until after passing Walltown. Two centurial stones have been built into the front wall of the farm-house; they are both much weathered. One seems to read >VALERI[I] VERI; the

Cockmount Hill.

Ollalee.

other, OMARIDI. About three furlongs beyond the mile-castle we reach Mucklebank-crag, the highest of the Nine Nicks of Thirlwall. It is 860 feet above the sea. The view is very extensive. In addition to the objects already named, the viaduct of the Alston Railway forms a pleasing feature in the landscape. The defile of Walltown-crags is a wide one. The fosse of the Wall is, as is usual in similar situations, strong. Mucklebank crag.

At Walltown several objects attract our attention. Nearest to the Wall is a spring, surrounded by masonry, now much disordered, called the King's Well; the present inhabitants call it King Arthur's Well. Other accounts are given of it. Hutchinson says—"Travellers are shown a well among the cliffs, where it is said Paulinus baptized King Egbert; but it is more probable it was Edwin, King of Northumberland." The well has no doubt been a place of historical interest and importance, but unhappily modern drainage is robbing it of its treasures. Another interesting circumstance is connected with this locality. In the crevices of the whin-rock near the house chives grow abundantly. The general opinion is, that we are indebted for these plants to the Romans, who were much addicted to the use of these and kindred vegetables. Most of the early writers refer to this subject; let the reader take a passage from Camden:—"The fabulous tales of the common people concerning this Wall, I doe wittingly and willingly overpasse. Yet this one thing which I was enformed of by men of good credit, I will not conceale from the reader. There continueth a settled perswasion among a great part of the people thereabout, and the same received by tradition, that the Roman soldiers of

Walltown.

The King's Well.

Tradition respecting Roman plants.

the marches did plant here every where in old time for their use certaine medicinable hearbs, for to cure wounds: whence is it that some emperick practitioners of chirurgery in Scotland, flock hither every year in the beginning of summer, to gather such simples and wound-herbes; the vertue whereof they highly commend as found by long experience, and to be of singular efficacy." (*Phil. Holland's*, p. 795.) Another point of interest here is the site of the Tower of Walltown, the inheritance of John Ridley, the brother of the martyr. The present farm-house is a modern erection. Only a fragment of the old castellated building remained in Wallis's time; even this is now gone. Mr. McLauchlan discerned "Faint traces of Tower" to the north-west of the present house. The old village of Walltown, which hung on the sunny slope near the Tower, has, also passed away. (*See Hodgson's North.*, II., iii., p. 324.) To the east of Walltown-house, on a small hill covered with fir trees, is an ancient camp, which reminds us that on Castle-hill, Haltwhistle. Mr. McLauchlan was of the first person to notice it.

The Nine Nicks of Thirlwall.

Leaving the valley, we climb a steep ascent, which soon brings us to the site of another mile-castle. This is a most interesting and peculiar part of the line. The mural ridge, divided by frequent breaks into as many isolated peaks, gives rise to the denomination of the Nine Nicks of Thirlwall. The view from the edge of the cliff is extensive, whilst stunted trees unite with the craggy character of the rock in giving variety to the foreground. The Wall climbs and descends the little hills unflinchingly, and adapts itself with its accustomed pertinacity to the ragged edges of the basaltic line. Its northern face occasionally shows a well-preserved specimen of the structure, as in the accompanying example.

Sir Walter Scott, who was familiar with this part of the Wall, probably here penned the lines:—

"TO A LADY WITH FLOWERS FROM THE ROMAN WALL.

"Take these flowers, which purple waving,
On the ruined rampart grew,
Where, the sons of freedom braving
Rome's imperial standards flew.

"Warriors from the breach of danger
Pluck no longer laurels there:
They but yield the passing stranger
Wild-flower wreaths for beauty's hair."

The general character of the scenery is shown in the next cut, which exhibits the line of the Wall as we see it looking eastward. At length the cliffs, which extend in a

nearly unbroken series from Sewingshields to Carvoran, sink into a plain, and the fertility and beauty of a well-cultivated country re-appear.

Magna—Carvoran.

The Station described.

CARVORAN is the Magna of the *Notitia*, where, according to that document, the second cohort of the Dalmatians was stationed. No inscriptions have been found corroborating this statement. The station is a little more than two miles and a half from Great Chesters, and it contains an area of 3½ acres. Its position is particularly strong. It is to the south both of Vallum and Wall, having probably been erected before them, by Agricola, in order to command the valley of the Tipalt. The numerous sharp turns which the

Vallum makes to avoid the bog on the north of the station, are inimical to Horsley's idea that the north agger of the Vallum was Agricola's military way. The interior of the station has in recent times been subjected to the plough; before this its ruins were stately. Stukeley says, "there were vestiges of houses and buildings all over, within and without." The outline of the station, which is to the west of the farm-house, may, though with difficulty, be made out; some portions of the north rampart remain, and the north fosse is distinct. Numerous memorials of Roman days are preserved in the farm-house. Fragments of columns, broken

Horsley's theory doubtful.

Outside of the Station.

Antiquities.

capitals, coping-stones, gutter-stones, troughs of various shape and size, mill-stones, and altars, are clustered together in heaps. In the house is a small altar inscribed to the local god BELATVCADER. Amongst the altars in the garden, is one inscribed I[OVI] O[PTIMO] M[AXIMO] HELIOPOLIS (?) The fragment of the body of another has on it the names of Calpurnius Agricola, a man of consular rank (see *Historical Data*, p. 7), and Licinius Clemens, a præfect. Built into the garden wall is a small altar ascribed to the local god VETERES, and a centurial stone marked with the name of SORION[IS]. An uninscribed altar is built into one angle of the farm-house. The Stanegate or direct Roman-way came in front of the station, and the Maiden-way, after traversing the wastes of Stanemoor and Alston, came up to its south-east angle. With Mr. McLauchlan's Survey in hand, the course of these roads may yet be traced.

The Direct Eastern and Western and the Great Southern.

The north fosse between Carvoran and Thirlwall Castle, is particularly well developed; the lines of the Vallum, running parallel with the Wall, may also be traced in their course to the little river Tipalt. In an outhouse at Holmhead a Roman inscribed stone is inserted. It may puzzle the uninitiated, in consequence of its being placed upside down. It reads CIVITAS DVMNONI. The Dumnonii were a British tribe occupying Devonshire and Cornwall. The castle of Thirlwall has some interesting features. The wood-cut will give an idea of its general appearance. It is entirely built of Wall stones.

Down to the Tipalt.

The Castle of Thirlwall.

It is generally stated that Thirlwall derives its name from the fact that here the Caledonians first *thirled* or threw down the *Wall*. *Thirl-ian* is an Anglo Saxon word, signifying to penetrate. Whatever truth there may be in this etymology, it is certain that this is the weakest part of the Wall. Camden has the following remark— "But this is worth the observation, that as by the wisdome of the Romans this Wall was so built, that it had two very great rivers neere to it on the inner side (as it were) for another defence, namely, Tine and Irthing, that are divided the one from the other with a very narrow parcell of ground: So on the other side the barbarous people were so cunning, that in the same place especially they made their first entrance betwixt these rivers, where they might have free passage farther into the heart of the Province, without hinderance of any river, according as we will shew by and by."

The weakest part of the Wall.

Closely adjoining Thirlwall Castle is the village of Glenwhelt. This name has a thoroughly Celtic sound. Mr. McLauchlan says:—"It is possibly British, from *Glynn*, a valley; and *whelt*, darkness; an appropriate name, from the precipitous nature of the ground." (*Mem.*, p. 49.) In the inn at Glenwhelt are a pair of red-deer's horns, taken out of the Roman well at Carvoran; and in a stone fence near is a much-weathered bust, that no doubt, once adorned the Roman camp.

Glenwhelt.

The railway station of Greenhead is close to Glenwhelt.

VI. From the Tipalt to the Eden.

No traces of the Wall and Vallum remain in the flat between Thirwall Castle and the railway, but both appear on the bank to the left of the railway. Before pursuing his journey further, the traveller had better examine a camp and the military-way (Stanegate), which he will find to the south of the lines, and very near the railway station. "The form of the camp is a rectangular parallelogram, having its east and west sides about 165 yards, and its north and south 88, giving an area of about 3 acres. It appears to have been an earthwork only, now nearly destroyed, except the east part of the north front; its entrances, and the whole outline, however, are visible. Each of the gates has had a straight traverse in front, together with that peculiar semicircular flexure of the rampart opposite the gateway, so frequently noticed in camps on the line of the Watling Street, and supposed by some persons to have been used by Agricola." (*Mem.* p. 49.) The Stanegate is on the north side of this camp. There is another smaller camp, of similar construction, about 5 furlongs to the west of this. These are the only two camps noticed by Mr. McLauchlan on the line of the Wall, having the peculiar defence of gateway referred to. Besides these two, there are other three camps, of the ordinary construction, lying to the south of the Wall, between the Tipalt and the Irthing. "We have thus," says Mr. McLauchan, "five camps between Carvoran and Birdoswald, at a mean distance from each other of about half-a-mile; occupying every prominent height on the south of the Wall, at a mean distance from it of about two furlongs and a half. We may fairly consider them as a third line of defence, along that part of the barrier where the natural defences of the ground were the weakest." (*Mem.* 52.)

Legionary camp.

Other temporary camps.

Wallend.

We now hurry on. Wallend is soon reached. The

earthworks are for a short distance in excellent preservation. Between Wallend and Chapel House, the fosse of the Wall is of unusually large dimensions. Here is a view of it. The Fosse of the Wall.

Before coming to Chapel House, traces of a mile-castle may be seen—as usual, beside a field gateway. Foultown is a farm-house contiguous to Chapel House. Chapel House and Foultown.

Built up in a stable at Chapel House, the stone represented in the margin was found. It is a dedication, on the part of the twentieth legion, to the Emperor Hadrian. At the village of Gap the Vallum, which is very distinct, stands considerably above the Wall. The summit of Rose Hill has been removed to Gap. Rose Hill.

afford a site for the railway station. Dr. Lingard's MS. notes (1807) have the following notice of it:—"A sugar-loaf hill, 200 yards from the Wall, called Rose Hill. It has a platform on the top 12 yards in diameter, with a ditch round it. Here was a figure of flying Victory." This sculptured stone is now at Rockliffe; a drawing of it is here introduced; it is exceedingly curious.

Figure of flying Victory.

Gilsland Spa

Gilsland Spa, a sulphur spring, is about a mile and a half distant from Rose Hill. Here is an excellent hostel which the pilgrim will probably visit; a brief digression may therefore be allowed. The banks of the Irthing in the immediate vicinity of the Spa are bold and rocky, and cannot fail to delight the visitor. A broad flat stone in the bed of the river, a little above the hotel, is called the "Popping-stone," from the circumstance that Sir Walter Scott put an important question to his subsequent wife, when they stood upon it—admiring the surrounding scenery. On our way to Gilsland Spa we pass Mumps Ha', formerly the residence of the Meg Merrilees of Sir Walter Scott. It is the house round which the road bends at a right angle before we reach the bridge

MumpsHall.

over the Irthing. The front of the building has been altered, but the back, which is shown here, retains its original cha-

racter. The house was an inn, and being at the edge of a waste which stretched into Scotland, was the only place within many miles where refreshment could be obtained. "Meg" was buried in Upper Denton church-yard. Her tombstone, which lies with its face on the ground, near that of her daughter, Margaret Teasdale, also of Mumps Hall, bears the following inscription:—"Mumps Hall. Here lies the body of Margarett Carrick ye Wife of Tho. Carrick who departed this life ye 4 of Decem. 1717 in the 100 year of her age."

Upper Denton.

We now revert to the Wall at Rose Hill. Between this point and Birdoswald it has some features of interest; but should the river Irthing not be easily fordable, the pilgrim may be induced to take the public road, which deviates considerably from the track of the Wall. The Birdoswald road

The Wall between Rose Hill and Irthing.

is the first to the left that we meet with on the road to Gilsland after crossing the bridge.

Taking the Wall on the south side of Rose Hill village, we find the earth-works in an encouraging state. Following them we come to the Poltross-burn, the boundary line between Northumberland and Cumberland. The gorge in which the stream flows is deep and well-wooded. No remains of a bridge appear. On the top of the western bank we meet with the marked vestiges of a mile-castle, which is 7¼ furlongs from the last, near Chapel House. The Wall now crosses the railway, and it is seen, two or three courses high, stretching westwards towards Willowford. The north fosse is strongly developed. On the flat ground bordering upon the river it cannot be distinctly traced; the hedge, amongst the roots of which are a number of Wall stones, probably indicates its course.

Poltross-burn.

How the Wall crossed the river, and ascended the cliff which bounds its western bank, no remains are left to show. Usually, in the summer season, passengers may cross the river dry-shod. On the summit of the cliff we meet with another mile-castle.

Amboglanna—Birdoswald.

The Station described.

We now approach BIRDOSWALD, the 12th station on the line. Its position is remarkably strong. In addition to the bold cliffs which guard it on the south, and at the foot of which the Irthing flows, a bold chasm on its northern boundary admits of the flow of the superfluous waters of the Midge-holm Bog into the Irthing. Its western side is its weakest. On the edge of this northern chasm, approaching the station, are some artificial lines of defence. It has been suggested that these are the remains of a Saxon or Danish fortress. Two small hills in this vicinity have the appearance of barrows; they are probably, however, the result of diluvial action.

The largest Station.

Birdoswald is nearly three miles and a quarter from Carvoran. It is the largest station on the line, having an area of 5½ acres, which is about a quarter of an acre more than Chesters, and half an acre more than Housesteads. It possesses the peculiarity of having two gates both in its eastern and western ramparts. Most of the camps of the Wall have a southern exposure; in this, the southern margin is slightly elevated above the rest of the ground; the northern half of the station is nearly level. A very great number of inscriptions have been found in the station, most of which confirm the *Notitia* statement that the first cohort of Dacians, styled the Ælian, was quartered here. One of them, which is here drawn, was found by Mr. Glassford Potter in

The Notitia compared with inscriptions.

excavating the upper gateway in the eastern rampart. The inscription may be translated:—"The first cohort of the Dacians (styled the Ælian), commanded by Marcus Claudius Menander the Tribune, [erected this] by direction of Modius Julius, Imperial Legate, and Proprætor." On one side of the slab is a palm branch, the emblem of victory; on the other is a sword of peculiar form. A reference to the Trajan column at Rome shews us that the Dacians used a curved sword. An example is here given.

Garrisoned by the Dacians.

It would hence appear that the Romans, in adopting the services of the various nations whom they subdued, allowed them the use of the accoutrements and arms with which they were most familiar. On three occasions lately, extensive excavations have been made in this station by Mr. H. Norman, the proprietor of the camp, Mr. W. S. Potter, and

Extensive excavations.

Mr. H. Glasford Potter. By this means the gateways of the station have been displayed, and some of the interior buildings. Mr. Glasford Potter has described the more important of these excavations in two papers in the last quarto volume of the *Archæologia Æliana.*

The walls of the station are in a good state of preservation; the southern rampart especially, which shows eight courses of facing-stones. The walls are five feet thick. The moat which surrounded the walls may also be satisfactorily traced. On the east side of the station are extensive and strong marks of suburban dwellings.

The walls of the station.

Suburbs.

Although the Wall adapts itself to the north rampart of the fort, the station is entirely independent of the Wall

Station independent of the Wall.

(as is shown in the wood-cut),* and must have been built

* Since this cut was prepared, that portion of the Wall which adjoined the station has been removed, to allow of a new entrance to the house.

before it. Probably, as has been already observed, the first step taken in the construction of the Barrier in every case was the erection of the stationary camps.

North gateway.

The north gateway has been destroyed, but the foundation of one of its jambs may sometimes be seen in the road in front of the station. A heap of ruins in the shrubbery

marks the site of the most northerly of the west gates. The other gateway on this side is shown in the wood-cut. It is a single gateway. Marks of ruts appear on its threshold; the pivot-holes remain.

West gateway.

South gateway.

The south gateway is a double one, and is a very noble specimen of Roman masonry. The plan of it is similar to that of the gateways at Housesteads, though its masonry is not so massive. The gateway is double. Each portal is eleven feet wide, and has been spanned by an arch. The pivot-holes are to be seen. The west portal has, at some period before the abandonment of the station, been closed, and converted into a dwelling-house; the stones with which it was floored remain. As usual, this gateway has two guard-chambers; the eastern one has not been excavated; the other, though excavated, has again become encumbered with its own ruins. Adjoining the west guard-chamber is another apartment; in one angle is a circular depression, bearing marks of fire The south-west angle of the station contains several buildings, which, if excavated, would no doubt display points of considerable interest.

Both of the gateways on the eastern side have been excavated. The lower one is much twisted and broken by the yielding of its foundations. The other gateway is in an excellent state of preservation. The accompanying sketch, which has necessarily been drawn to a minute scale, shows it. This

The east gate.

gateway is a double one, and is provided with guard-chambers on each side. The plan of it nearly resembles that of the gateways at Housesteads. As usual, one of the portals (the north) had been closed with large stones. Some traces of a second floor will be noticed, raised about a foot above the original one. This is in consistency with the signs of hasty reparation which we meet with throughout the line.

The pivot-holes remain, and in the threshold of the northern portal is a large stone, against which the leaves of the gate closed. Several circular door-heads were found in the vicinity of this and the other gateways. The accompanying wood-cut, shewing the northern entrance into the guard-chamber, indicates the use to which they were applied. These door-heads are always found thrown down and often broken.

Interior of station.

The whole interior of the camp is marked with the lines of streets and the ruins of buildings. Near the lower gateway in the east wall three chambers, of nine or ten feet square each, have been laid bare. One of them is furnished

Mother goddess.

with a hypocaust. Here was found the figure represented on the opposite page, which is now in the farm-house with

the exception of the head, which had been discovered thirty years previously, and is in the Museum at Newcastle. The figure is of the kind usually called *deæ matres*.

Large chambers.

In 1859 Mr. Norman, in levelling the broken ground in front of the farm-house, to form a new garden, came upon a very perfect specimen of a Roman building of large dimensions. A wall, 3½ feet thick, was found, extending 92 feet from east to west. This wall has not been excavated to the bottom; but it has been proved to be upwards of eight feet iu height. It is supported by eight buttresses. In the middle of the space between each buttress is a long slit or loop-hole. These perforations are supposed to be connected with the flues used in warming the building. Immediately in front of this wall is another of similar thickness. Three other walls were found to the north of the main one. Until the entire building be laid bare (of which there is no immediate prospect), it will be difficult to form a correct idea of its arrangements and uses.

Minor antiquities.

Many roofing-slates were found amongst the rubbish, some of them perforated with nail-holes. A few coins were discovered, belonging to the reigns of Vespasian, Domitian, Hadrian, Antoninus Pius, Marcus Aurelius, and Diocletian.

Some excavations were made here, at the expense of the Archæological Institute, when it met in Carlisle. A spot

Water-tank.

near the centre of the station, which always had a damp appearance, was cut down upon. The remains of a tank or reservoir for supplying the station with water were found. Some arrangements for filtering the water, by making it pass through a wall of charcoal, were noticed.

Water-course.

Shortly after this, Mr. Parker, of Brampton, discovered that this cistern was fed by a spring on the west side of the station. The water-course conducting the water to the tank was formed of flat stones set up on end, covered over by a third on the top; the whole was sunk in the ground. The writer was shown it at a distance of about 300 yards from the station; the water was then flowing in it.

Inscribed stones.

Several inscribed stones remain here. A broken and defaced altar lies in the station. It has been described both by Gordon and Horsley. It seems to be a dedication to the standards (SIGNIS) of the cohort. An altar to Fortune was found on re-building the farm-house; it has been ruthlessly treated in order to fit it for use as a building-stone. Another rudely-carved altar, once built into the farm-house, is dedicated to Jupiter, the best and greatest, by the first cohort of Dacians, which at this time, besides the epithet of Ælian, derived from Hadrian, seems to have had that of Tetrician derived from the Emperor Tetricus. (*Horsley, Cumb.*, vii.) There is here also the head of another altar, dedicated to Jupiter, having on the capital above the dedicatory letters (I. O. M.) a series of crosses, one of them being of that peculiar form called "gammadion." 
A stone broken across the middle has on it the inscription—

LEG. VI. VIC.
FIDELIS.

Centurial stones.

intimating that the sixth legion, styled the victorious and faithful, took part in the erection of the building in which it was inserted. Here also are several wall-stones, on which are inscribed the names of the centuries engaged in its erection in this vicinity. One of them imports that the troop (of a hundred men) had been commanded by Congaonus Candiorus; another bears the name of the Centuria

Hortensiana; and a third commemorates the century of Probianus, belonging to the fourth cohort.

The view of Troy.

Before taking leave of the station, we must notice the prospect both to the north and the south of us. The Earl of Carlisle, in his *Diary in Turkish and Greek Waters*, p. 87, says:—"Strikingly, and to any one who has coasted the uniform shore of the Hellespont, and crossed the tame low plain of the Troad, unexpectedly lovely is this site of Troy, if Troy it was. I could give any Cumberland borderer the best notion of it, by telling him that it wonderfully resembles the view from the point just outside the Roman camp at Birdoswald: both have that series of steep conical hills, with rock enough for wildness and verdure enough for softness; both have that bright trail of a river creeping in and out with the most continuous indentations: the Simois has, in summer at least, more silvery shades of sand." The view

VIEW FROM THE ROAD NORTH OF BIRDOSWALD.

to which his lordship refers is that which is obtained by a spectator who stands upon the edge of the cliff fronting the south rampart of the station.

We now take our stand on the road skirting the north wall of the station. Looking towards the north-west, we see (as shown in the cut) a tower-like object; it is a fragment of the walls of Triermain Castle, a building celebrated by Scott, in his "Bride of Triermain." But more to our present purpose;—the Maiden-way, which came up to the south rampart of Carvoran, seems to have proceeded northwards from this station right over the hills before us, past Bewcastle, and so into Scotland. On the top of a distant hill, called Gillalees Beacon, nearly due north, a small cairn-like object may be discerned, in favourable states of the atmosphere. This is the ruin of a Roman watch-tower by the side of the Maiden-way. Between Birdoswald and the river King-water, the traces of the road are somewhat dubious; but after crossing this river and coming to Ash Fell, a strip of the Way is met with in a nearly perfect state. Having once fallen in with the road, the antiquary may, without much difficulty, trace it very nearly to Bewcastle. Beyond Bewcastle its course is dubious.

Triermain Castle.

The Maiden-way.

Roman watch-tower.

We now follow the Wall westward from Birdoswald. The Wall in this part is in an unusually good state of preservation. It is 7½ feet thick. Some portions of it, however, are beginning to exhibit evident signs of decrepitude and decay. On the south side of the Wall, in the second field from the station, are the remains of what seem to be the side walls of a turret; these fragments of walls are three feet thick. The building measures 13 feet from side to side, inside measure-

Probable remains of a turret.

ment. These remains are feeble, but they are interesting, as being the first distinct traces that we have met with of a turret. At the distance of little more than half a mile from the station we come to the site of another mile-castle. The fosse of the Wall and the earthworks of the Vallum here form interesting objects of study. In this part of its course the Vallum is strengthened on its northern side by a second ditch. This additional defence begins to appear shortly after we leave Birdoswald, and it terminates abruptly at the next mile-castle, that of Wallbours. It is difficult to divine its object.

A second Fosse to the Vallum.

After passing a cottage called Apple Trees, the Wall and Vallum draw towards each other, until, on the top of the next summit, where the Wallbours mile-castle stands, they are in tolerably close proximity. After this they run parallel to each other for some distance. The supplementary fosse ceases at the Wallbours castellum.

Wallbours.

The inscriptions at Coome-crag.

Arriving at a lodge on the traveller's left hand, a path leads to Coome-crag, a red freestone quarry, which has been extensively wrought by the Romans. The workmen have left some inscriptions on the face of the rock, amongst which may perhaps be discerned the names SECVRVS, IVSTVS, MATHRIANVS. Some unhappy individual, fancying that a coat of paint was necessary to preserve from decay inscriptions which had defied the storms of seventeen centuries, has bedaubed them all with white—thereby destroying their antique character. At the foot of the cliff is an inscription which, fortunately, he of the paint-pot did not at the time know of. It reads (though some of the letters are in ligature)—

FAVST. ET RVF. COS.

Faustinus and Rufus were consuls A.D. 210. Curiously enough, whilst the rock in the immediate vicinity of this inscription is covered with a smoke-coloured lichen, the letters themselves are covered with a white lichen; this renders them very distinct.

Nothing will occur to arrest attention until we arrive at Banks-head. There were formerly the remains of a mile-castle here; but the pilgrim will have some difficulty in detecting them now. In 1808 two altars to the local deity Cocidius, which are now at Lanercost, were discovered at Banks-head.

The Wall next goes over a small hill called Pike. Here was discovered last year (1862) a broken slab, bearing the name of Antoninus Pius. The next group of houses is called Banks, or Banks-hill. The view from this point of the fertile plains below is exceedingly striking. The Pike.

Before coming to the brook called Banks-burn, a piece of the core of the Wall is seen. Ascending the hill on the western side of the brook, is a fragment of the Wall, which stands 9 feet 10 inches high. It is, however, divested of its facing-stones. Hutton, speaking of it, says:—"I viewed this relic with admiration. I saw no part higher." Just beyond this piece of Wall is the still distinguishable site of a mile-castle. Hare Hill.

Lanercost and Naworth.

At this point of our progress the antiquary may be disposed to forsake the Wall for a while, to view two relics of the mediæval period of great interest—Lanercost Priory and Naworth Castle. Before reaching Lanercost, a rock Mediæval degression.

inscription may be seen on the face of a limestone quarry, overhanging Banks-burn. Divested of its ligatures, it reads:

I. BRVTVS
DEC. AL. PET.

—Junius Brutus, a decurion of the Petriana Ala, or wing of horse. Lanercost Priory was founded by Robert de Vallibus, Lord of Gilsland, and intended for the comfort of the canons regular of the order of St. Austin. The church was consecrated in the year 1169. In 1296 the monastery suffered from an invasion of the Scottish forces. During the winter of 1306 and 1307 King Edward I. resided with his queen in the monastery, and in consequence of the expense to which he had put the fraternity, and in consideration of the damage which they had sustained by the invasion of the Scots, he granted them the advowsons of two churches in his patronage. The spirit of the "*Venatores Bannæ*" (to be afterwards alluded to) was occasionally strong in the holy brotherhood. Thomas de Hextoldesham, who was elected Prior in 1357, was obliged, by the Bishop, to make a solemn promise that he would not frequent public huntings, or keep so large a pack of hounds as he had formerly done. On the suppression of the monasteries, the priory and adjacent lands were granted to a branch of the Dacre family. In consequence of the failure of male issue, in 1716 the lands reverted to the crown, and are now held on lease by the Earl of Carlisle. Of the priory church the only portion which is in repair is the nave, and this is used as a parish church. It has recently been renovated. The buildings are partly Norman, but mostly early English, of an early and massive design. The western elevation is

Foundation of the Priory.

Its suppression.

exceedingly chaste and beautiful. It is, however, pitted with bullet-marks. This was not done by Oliver Cromwell, as has sometimes been said, but by the loyal Cumberland volunteers, who, when, at the beginning of this century, Buonaparte threatened to invade England, shouldered the musket and practised upon the church. The choir and transepts, which are roofless, present some singular and beautiful combinations of very early date. Here are several large tombs. One is the resting-place of Humfrey Dacre and Mabell his wife; the latter dying in 1509. Another is attributed to Sir Humfrey's son Thomas, the second Lord Dacre, who married Elizabeth, the heiress of Greystock, and who died in 1525. Another records the death, in 1716, of the last male heir of the Dacres of Lanercost. Monumental remains.

Several of the monastic buildings remain. The site of the cloisters is an open space used as a garden. The refectory was on the south side of the cloisters, parallel with the church. Its walls are thrown down, but the vaulted cellars, upon which the refectory was usually placed, remain. At the west end of the vault is a door-way, which led up into the refectory. The dormitory was on the west side of the cloister; it is often taken for the refectory, in consequence of a large fire-place having been inserted in it by Christopher Dacre of Lanercost, son of Thomas Dacre, the grantee. It is marked "C. D. 1586." At the angle formed by the union of the dormitory and refectory was the prior's own mansion. It is now deserted. There are other monastic buildings exhibiting the usual dog-tooth ornament of the period. (See *Arch. Æl.*, N.S., vol. iv., p. 147.) The conventual buildings.

The priory, church, and monastic buildings are almost

Has there been a station here?

entirely composed of Roman stones. These may have been procured from the Wall; but the mind can scarcely divest itself of the idea that there has been a station here. There are some indications of ramparts and of a north gateway in the priory-green. A little excavation would determine the point.

Centurial stones.

There are some Roman inscribed and sculptured stones here. At the door of the farm-house occupied by Mr. Coulthard, is a centurial stone, which may probably be read—The century of Claudius Priscus. In the west wall of the cloister-garth is another, which may be translated—The century of Cassius Priscus. In the headway of the clerestory, in the south-east angle of the choir, is an altar, which was first described in the *Gentleman's Magazine*, for 1744. The inscription on it may be translated—"To Jupiter, the best and greatest, the first cohort of the Dacians, styled the Ælian, commanded by Julius Saturninus the tribune [dedicates this.]" In the vault are several interesting antiquities. One of them, an altar dedicated by the hunters of Banna to the holy god Silvanus, is exceedingly curious, as indicating the mode in which the officers of the Roman army sought to relieve the tedium of their leisure hours. It is as yet an unsolved question where Banna was; it must have been in this neighbourhood. The

Altar to Silvanus.

next altar is one of those found in the Banks-head mile-castle; it reads—"To the god Cocidius, the soldiers of the legion, styled the Valerian and the Victorious, dedicate this altar, in discharge of a vow to an object most worthy of it in the consulship of Aper and Rufus." The boar at the foot is the emblem of the twentieth legion. One other illustration is all that our space will allow. It is a somewhat spirited representation of Jupiter and Hercules. A metal thunderbolt (probably gilt) was no doubt inserted in the hole in the right hand of Jupiter.

Altar to Cocidius.

Sculpture of Jupiter and Hercules.

Roman bridge over the Irthing.

A little below the present bridge, and immediately opposite the priory, are the remains of a Roman bridge. In the river the wooden frame-work on which one of the piers has been founded is visible when the water is low. Another pier, which has been deserted by the river, and is deprived of its facing-stones, is ten feet high. About forty feet beyond this are the remains of what appears to have been the land abutment, on the north side of the river. There are some traces of a road on the south side of the Irthing.

Naworth Castle.

Ascending the rising ground south of the river, we soon come to Naworth Castle. Some magnificent oak trees stand near the entrance gateway, on which, tradition says, Belted Will used to hang the luckless moss-troopers who fell into his power. In this instance there can be little doubt that tradition errs. The castle is strongly posted on the edge of a platform, nearly insulated by a deep gully. The first possessor of Naworth that we have any account of was a Dacre, who filled the office of sheriff for Cumberland in 1236. In 1316 Ralph Neville obtained a license from Edward II. to castellate his mansion at Naworth, and to this period most of the buildings must be referred. (*Rev. C. Hartshorne, Newcastle Vols. of Arch. Inst.*, vol. ii., p. 76.) In 1569 the great inheritance of the Dacres was divided, passing into the hands of three sisters, coheiresses. The barony of Gilsland fell to the lot of Elizabeth—"Bessie with the braid apron"—who married Lord William Howard, third son of the Duke of Norfolk. This is the Belted Will of traditional lore. He was made Warden of the Marches in the reign of Elizabeth, and, by his vigorous proceedings, reduced this turbulent district to order.

Belted Will.

This Border fortress chiefly consists of two large square towers, united by other buildings, and inclosing a quadrangular court. Until seriously injured by fire in 1844, the castle remained nearly in the state in which Belted Will left it. Pennant's description was then strictly applicable:—"The whole house is a true specimen of ancient inconvenience, of magnificence and littleness; the rooms numerous, accessible by sixteen staircases, with frequent sudden ascents and descents into the bargain; besides a long narrow gallery." The restoration of the building has been carefully effected, and it retains much that is interesting to the student of antiquity. The great hall is redolent of heraldic pomp—the Greystock dolphin, the Howard calf, and the Dacre bull and griffin being made use of to support the banners of the house. The walls are 7½ feet thick; the fire-place has a span of 15½ feet. In the hall we have two complete suits of armour, one of which Belted Will was himself in the habit of wearing. A painting of Lord William and his lady are among the pictorial treasures of the place; they were fortunately in the Polytechnic Exhibition at Newcastle at the time of the fire. Here, too, are some good pieces of tapestry. The private apartments of Lord William, and the careful manner in which he guarded the approach to them, are worthy of observation. A concealed passage leading from his oratory to a grated aperture at the top of the principal dungeon, where he might, without being observed, listen to the conversation of his prisoners, is amongst the curious arrangements of the place. The dungeons themselves and all their apparatus are unmistakably genuine.

The great hall.

The dungeons.

South of Naworth Castle, and near the railway, is an ancient earthwork, probably British. "It has two encircling ramparts." (*McL. Mem.*, p. 60.)

British camp.

At Naworth-gate the trains on the Newcastle and Carlisle Railway stop to take up or set down passengers, on notice being given.

Return to the Wall. We now rejoin the Wall at Hare Hill. A little beyond the mile-castle a break in the Wall occurs, in which a turret or small quadrangular building has been situated. This building projects beyond the Wall, northwards, rather less than three feet. It is constructed of smaller stones than the Wall; the workmanship of it is excellent. It measures 14 feet 6 inches (inside measurement) from east to west. When first noticed, it was full of black ashes; the discoverers took it to be a smithy. A turret? Altogether it is a peculiar building; though it has some of the features of a turret, it seems to have been built independently of the Wall. At Money Holes attempts have been made to discover treasure; Money Holes. no doubt in vain. Through the priory-woods, to the south of us, the works of the Vallum proceed undauntedly on their onward course, and are in good condition. The fact that the Vallum goes along the southern slope of the hill, leaving the summit to the Wall, bears upon the question of the contemporaneous or successive construction of the works.

At Craggle Hill the north fosse is very bold. At Hayton Gate a drove-road, closed half a century ago, crossed the Wall. Randelands. A very little west of Randelands we meet with the feeble traces of a mile-castle. After crossing the rivulet, called Burtholme Beck, a piece of the Wall is seen, which stands nearly seven feet high; its facing-stones are gone, but the rough pebbly mortar possesses its original tenacity. As is often the case, the ruin is tufted with hazel bushes, oak trees, and alders. Beyond this point a second ditch and rampart, outside the Wall, seem, for a short distance, to have been added to the usual lines of fortification. The Howgill. Wall passes on the north of Howgill, Low Wall, and Dovecote on its way to the King-water. In the rear of the farm-house at Howgill is a rude inscription, mentioned by Horsley and all subsequent antiquaries, which seems to record the achievements of a British tribe, the Catuvellauni. Tacitus tells us that Agricola took southern Britons with him to the battle of the Grampians; Hadrian and Severus may have been similarly accompanied in their expeditions. Nearly due north of Low Wall are slight indications of a mile-castle. The prickly enclosures of the fields may prevent all but very zealous antiquaries keeping very close companionship with the Wall for a little distance; those who take the road by Dovecote will be brought back to their old friend before crossing the King-water.

Westward of the King-water, the village of Walton is reached; many of the stones of the Wall may be detected in its cottages. The Vallum is here indistinct, and some distance from the Wall. At the entrance of the village faint traces of a mile-castle are to be observed. On the green to the west of the church, Horsley saw traces of an earthen camp, which was probably occupied by the troops, when building the Wall. At Sandysike farm-house, besides the foundations of the Wall, a few sculptured Roman stones are to be seen. We now descend into the valley of the Cambeck, having the north fosse for our guide. The next mile-castle must have stood either on the west side of the Cambeck-water or at Cambeck-hill; most likely the latter; all traces of it are obliterated.

Walton.

Sandysike.

Walton House.

The station described.

To reach Walton House station, it is best to turn off at Sandysike. The station stands to the south both of Wall and Vallum. Its situation is strong. On the north the ground falls precipitously towards the river Cambeck; on the south and west it slopes gently towards the Irthing. The station contains an area of $2\frac{3}{4}$ acres; it is distant from the station of Birdoswald about seven miles, an unusually long distance. As its site has long been used as a garden, its exact outline is considerably obscured. The traces of the ditch are visible, particularly on the west front. Professor Carlisle gives us an account of the digging up of this station (in 1791), in the *Archæologia*, vol. xi., and of the overthrow of the Wall in its vicinity. His account of the Wall will remind the reader of what he saw at Steel-rig. "As the remains of the Vallum itself [Murus] for near half a mile were entirely dug up, Mr. Johnstone, to whom the estate belongs, had an opportunity of examining the construction of this curious remnant of Roman industry with the greatest accuracy. Of this he gave me the following account:—The breadth of the foundation was eight feet; the Wall, where entire, was faced with large stones on both sides, and the space between them filled with rubbish-stone to the depth of a foot; then a strong cement of lime and sand, about four inches thick; over that a foot of rubbish, and then a cover of cement as before; these layers were succeeded by others of rubbish and cement alternately, till the interstice between the facing-stones was filled up to

The construction of the Wall.

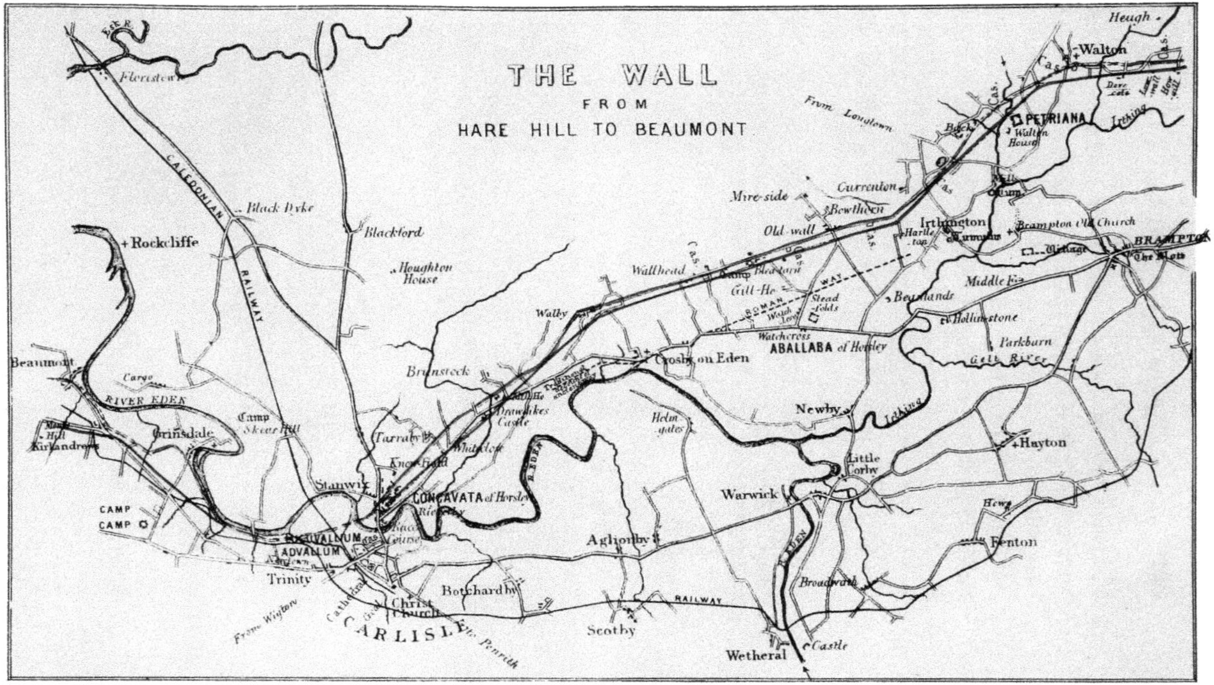
THE WALL
FROM
HARE HILL TO BEAUMONT
Heugh
Walton
PETRIANA
Walton House
Irthing
From Longtown
Currenton
Mire-side
Bowthorn
Irthington
Brampton Old Church
BRAMPTON
The Mote
Old wall
Wallhead
Gill-He
ROMAN WAY
Stead-folds
Beanlands
Middle Fa
Hollinstone
Parkburn
Gelt River
Watchcross
ABALLABA of Horsley
Crosby on Eden
Walby
Brunstock
Drawdikes Castle
Whiteclose
Tarraby
Know Field
Stanwix
CONCAVATA of Horsley
R. EDEN
Helm gates
Newby
Irthing
Little Corby
Hayton
Warwick
Hews
Fenton
Aglionby
Broadwath
Botchardby
RAILWAY
Scotby
Wetheral
Castle
EDEN
Trinity
Christ Church
Cathedral
CARLISLE
To Penrith
From Wigton
ADVALLUM
CAMP
CAMP
Kirkandrews
Grinsdale
Camp
Skeer Hill
Cargo
RIVER EDEN
Beaumont
Rockcliffe
Black Dyke
Blackford
Houghton House
CALEDONIAN
RAILWAY
Floristown
Esk R.

the top, and thus the whole became one solid cemented mass." Several valuable altars and other antiquities have been found in the station, most of which are carefully preserved on the spot by the present proprietor, W. Ponsonby Johnson, Esq. The most remarkable is the altar here

drawn. It has been translated :—"To Jupiter, the best and greatest, the second cohort of Tungrians, a miliary regiment, having a proportionate supply of horse, and consisting Altar to Jupiter.

of Roman citizens, commanded by Albus Severus, prefect of the Tungrians, erected this; the work being superintended by Victor Severus, the princeps." Here is a figure

An altar to Hadrian.

of Fortune; and here is a priest vested in his cope, and holding an incense-box in his hand. The altar inscribed DISCIPVLINAE AVGVSTI is very curious. The piety, the chastity, the constancy, and other moral qualities of the emperors, were often deified; but it was not usual to rear altars to their administrative qualities. But on the reverse of several of the coins of Hadrian we have the legend DISCIPLINA AVG., with a suitable device. The next cut shows

one. There can be little doubt that the Augustus referred

to on this altar is Hadrian. He maintained a severe discipline.

Petriana at Walton House? The *Notitia Imperii* places a troop of cavalry at Petriana, called the *Ala Petriana*. Unhappily we have not found, at Walton House, any traces of this body of horse.

Difficulties. Westward of Birdoswald no inscriptions have been found to enable us to identify the stations with any thing like certainty. To render conjecture doubly futile, antiquaries are not perfectly agreed as to what localities in this neighbourhood are to be ranked as "*stationes per lineam Valli.*" The scarcity of stone in Cumberland, and the general richness of the soil, has led to the demolition of some of them before accurate observations were made.

We now rejoin the Wall on the west bank of the Cambeck, and will follow it without interruption to Stanwix. Having done this, we will return and view the camps that have been noticed south of both lines of the Barrier. It will be observed how deeply the fosse of the Wall has been cut into the red sandstone rock forming the western bank of the stream. The fosse of the Vallum is also discernible a little lower down. Cambeck-hill. Cambeck-hill farm-house is passed. The farm-buildings at Beck are partially constructed of Roman stones, and on the east side of the rivulet a few stones of the Wall are in their original position.

Headswood. Headswood, as its name implies, occupies a commanding situation. The ditch, both of Wall and Vallum, are seen as you approach it. There are some works here on

the north side of the fosse. Mr. McLauchlan thinks that they may perhaps be the remains of one of those camps with a round elevated part, which are thought to have a Saxon or Danish origin. (*Mem.*, p. 70.) About 200 yards
White Flat west of the Newtown of Irthington, we meet with evident traces of a mile-castle. We next come to White Flat, where the rubble of the foundation of the Wall is very discernible, and the ditch very deep. The pilgrim who wishes to keep by the Wall will avoid the cart-road which takes to Irthington, and follow the footpath which runs through the fields. Westward of White Flat the works are feeble, but we soon meet with a long strip of the Wall, in an encouraging state; it is planted with oak trees; the north fosse shows nobly.
Hurtleton. We now pass Hurtleton, leaving it a little to the south. Here the Wall and Vallum are but 35 yards apart; the fosse of each is distinct. Both works now bend northwards. About mid-way between this point and Old Wall a mile-castle once stood; the traces are very faint, but the ruins of the building raise it somewhat above the general level. In
Old Wall. the buildings at Old Wall many Roman stones will be noticed; in a stable is a centurial stone, bearing an inscription which may be translated:—"The century of Julius Tertullia, belonging to the second legion, styled the August." The Wall is here entirely uprooted, many hundred cart-loads of stone having been removed within living memory; but the fosse of the Wall is visible between the road-way and the houses. From this point westward the works may be traced for some distance with satisfaction, an ancient drove-road running upon the site of the Wall. At the end of this lane, tall hedges and cultivated fields interfere ma-

terially with the pilgrim's progress. At a spot called High Strand there ought to be a mile-castle; tradition says that there once was one here.

Bleatarn is a place of considerable interest. The Wall runs a little to the north of the farm-house; the Vallum is immediately south of it. Between the Wall and the Vallum, and westward of the farm-house, is a large tumulus, which has been considerably diminished in height within the last few years. The site of the Wall here rises above the general surface. Bleatarn.

Before coming to Wallhead there ought, judging by the distance, to be a mile-castle. About 600 yards before we reach Walby, there are faint signs of a mile-castle, being 7½ furlongs from the last; they are where the road turns sharply to the north. At Walby there are some pools in the north fosse. Here the Wall bends strongly to the south. At Wall Foot there has probably been a mile-castle. "The place for the next mile-castle would fall opposite to Drawdikes Castle." (*Mem.*, p. 73.) Immediately in front of Drawdikes Castle the lines of the Vallum are clearly discernible, though the mounds have been lowered of late, to make the place more sightly. The three busts on the top of Drawdikes Castle are said to have come from the Wall; and yet, with strange perversity, they are believed to represent the devil and two local celebrities, one of them a modern lawyer. On close inspection they will be found to have nothing Roman about them. Built into the wall at the back of the house is a monumental stone, which, according to Horsley, was brought from Stanwix. The inscription may be read:—"To the Divine Manes of Marcus Trojanus

Wallhead. Walby. Drawdikes.

Augustinius; his beloved wife, Ælia Amilla Lusima, caused this tomb to be erected."

Approach to Stanwix.

The Wall now makes straight for Stanwix. As we approach this place, the advantageous nature of its position as a Roman station is seen. A fine elevated platform is observed, having the church at its eastern boundary. The ground falls from it on every side except the west, and here the river, with its wide and precipitous valley, is close at hand. For some distance before coming to Stanwix, a rural road runs along the site of the Wall; the ditch to the north of it appears, but it has been much filled up within living memory.

Stanwix.

Position of the station.

The church and church-yard of Stanwix occupy the site of the station which guarded the northern bank of the Eden.

The station is upwards of eight miles from the station at Walton House. The outlines of it are not well defined, but Mr. McLauchlan, from the information which he was able to obtain, came to the conclusion that it contained an area of 2½ acres. No inscriptions have been found here to inform us what troops were in garrison in Roman times. In pulling down the old church, to make way for the present structure, a figure of Victory was found, which is now at Newcastle. Between the station and the north bank of the river Eden the fosse of the Wall is distinctly marked, and a hollow line, formed by the excavation of the foundation of the Wall itself, shows its track to the water's edge, near Hyssop Holme Well. Here for the present we must leave it.

The Wall. reaches the Eden.

Brampton, Irthington, and Watch Cross.

Subsidiary exploration.

The distance between Walton House and Stanwix renders the presumption strong that there was some Roman stronghold between them. Two places have been thought likely—Brampton Park and Watch Cross; but as they can be visited better from the line of the road between Brampton and Carlisle than from the line of the Wall, we have reserved a notice of them to this place. We will now commence our subsidiary exploration at Brampton. This little

Brampton.

manufacturing town was once upon the main line of road between Newcastle and Carlisle. The natural route for the railway was along the valley in which it lies. So violent, however, was the opposition of the inhabitants (yielding to ill-advice), that the railway company were constrained, at a greatly increased cost, to take their line up the southern ridge of the valley. Brampton suffers accordingly. The only ancient feature belonging to Brampton is the Mote, at the east end of the town. It consists of a natural elevation, which has no doubt been, at different periods, applied to defensive purposes. The small platform at the top was formerly "defended by a breastwork;" lower down a rampart and fosse still appear. This hill-post may have given origin to the town. About a mile and a half west of Brampton is the old church of Brampton, of which only the chancel remains. It is composed of Roman stones. In some recent excavations (1863), traces of a Roman road have been found, and some coins and pottery. On a gentle eminence to the south of the old church, are the fast-fading remnants of a Roman station. A century ago the site was covered with brushwood, and by this means escaped the attention of Horsley. The late Mr. Robert Bell, of the Nook, Irthington—a warm-hearted and intelligent antiquary—had, in early life, assisted in carting away the stones of its ramparts. His subsequent observations, communicated to Mr. Hodgson, Mr. McLauchlan, Mr. Roach Smith, and the writer, render it clear that the Romans had a camp here. Mr. McLauchlan estimates its area at an acre and a half. It is about a mile and a half from the station at Walton House. A large jar full of Roman coins was found near

The Mote.

Brampton Old Church.

this place in 1826. The coins were of a late date, extending from the time of Decius to that of Florianus. In the meadow below this camp, are several remarkable barrows. They probably belong to the Romano-Britannic period; but the spade and pickaxe alone can decide the point. Discovery of coins.

Irthington. Irthington, a village that lies to the west of the Irthing, and situated about mid-way between the river and the Wall, has two objects of interest for the antiquary. A castle stood here in Norman, and perhaps, also, in Saxon times. Nothing is left but the mound, on which probably a stronghold, most likely of timber, was reared. The church, a Transition-Norman building, is worth attention. It has recently been restored. The old structure consisted entirely of Roman stones. This church has doubtless often been the scene of fierce Border encounters before the union of the kingdoms. The columns were marked by fire, and numerous skeletons, lying in disorder, were found within the area.

Watch Cross. Nearly due south from Bleatarn, and close to the turnpike-road leading from Brampton to Carlisle, is the site of Watch Cross, another Roman camp. The boundaries of the station are now scarcely discernible, and all traces of building are entirely removed. It has contained an area of an acre and a half. (*McL.*, p. 72.) Little can be gleaned by a visit to it. We now return to the Eden at Stanwix.

Carlisle.

Mediæval digression. After crossing the river, the Wall, instead of proceeding straight to the castle, kept a course more to the west, and, passing over the flat, made for a spot near the engine-house at Newtown, which was used in supplying the canal (now converted into a railway) with water. (*McL. Mem.*, p. 75.) The Vallum, however, is supposed to have passed on the south side of the castle. (*Mem.*, p. 77.)

The ancient name of Carlisle.

All antiquaries agree that Carlisle is the *Luguvallium* of the Romans; but it does not occur in the list given in the *Notitia.* Up to a comparatively recent period, the Roman features of this city were very marked. Stukeley, writing in 1725, says—"Fragments of squared stones appear in every quarter of the city, and several square wells of Roman workmanship. At the present day, whenever an excavation is made, articles of Roman make are turned up."

Recent discoveries.

During the formation of the city sewers in 1854, Samian ware, coins, and various bronze articles were found in great quantities. The cut represents a Judæa Capta of Vespasian,

which was found on this occasion. It is striking to turn up in British soil, deposited in Roman times, such testimonies of the fulfilment of prophecy. (*Deut.*, xxviii., 49.)

The Castle.

The castle and the cathedral will repay the attention of the mediæval antiquary. Carlisle being situated so near the borders of Scotland, its castle was a building of great importance. William Rufus visited Carlisle in 1092, and took measures for rearing a fortress here. "The general figure of this keep, and of the encircling walls, are probably identical with those planned by Rufus." The foundations are, for the most part, composed of Roman stones. "David King of Scotland, took possession of the castle in 1135, and died here in 1153. In 1173 it was besieged by William the Lion; it was visited by Henry II. in 1186; surrendered to Alexander of Scotland in 1216; was retaken by the English in the following year, and has since continued in the hands of the English crown. Edward I. carried on extensive repairs in the castle, under the direction of John de Halton, bishop of Carlisle. This monarch made the castle his residence when he assembled his parliaments at Carlisle. Here his son received the homage of the nobility immediately after his father's death." During the reign of Edward III., also, extensive repairs were made. (*Rev. C. H. Hartshorne, Arch. Inst. Journal,* 1859, p. 338.) Mary Queen of Scots was, on her coming into England, confined in Carlisle Castle. The apartments which she occupied are now destroyed; the staircase alone remains. A rude table, at which it is said she sat, is shown. In 1745 the city and castle fell into the hands of the Pretender. On the suppression of the rebellion, many of the persons involved in it were imprisoned in the castle; traces of them yet remain, in the coats of arms, names, and sentences which they carved on the walls of their dungeons.

Mary Queen of Scots.

The Cathedral of Carlisle, is an interesting building. The nave, the south transept, portions of the north transept, and the lower part of the tower are the earliest parts; they belong to a church commenced by Walter, a Norman fol-

The Cathedral.

lower of the Conqueror in 1092, and completed in 1101, by Henry I. These parts are of the simplest and most massive type of Norman architecture. No portions of the Norman choir remain. The present choir was probably commenced by Bishop Silvester de Everdon, who came to the diocese in 1245, when the early English style had developed itself. At that time there seems to have been a project for rebuilding the whole Cathedral, and this will explain the position of the choir in regard to the nave and tower. The choir is twelve feet wider than the nave. Want of funds arrested the rise of the building when the tops of the main arches had been reached, and it was temporarily roofed in. Before the work was recommenced, a fire had occurred in

Progress of the building.

1292. When the work was resumed it went on slowly, and the utmost economy was used. The portions left uninjured by the fire were allowed to stand, and the old materials were used as far as they would go. Bishop Welton (1352-1362), and his successor, Thomas de Appleby, seem to have carried on the work vigorously, and to have completed the choir, including the wooden roof, before the death of Edw. III. By this time the Decorated style of architecture had become established in England, and was of course followed by these builders. The great

The east window.

east window, if it be not the very finest decorated window in existence, is rivalled only by the west window at York. There is some old glass in the upper portion of the window; the rest is by Hardman, and is in memory of the late Bishop Percy. The north transept was burnt in 1292, and again in 1390. After the last fire it was rebuilt, in the reign of Henry V., by Bishop Strickland, who also erected the upper part of the tower. At this period, it is almost needless to remark, the Perpendicular style prevailed. The whole building has recently been renovated by the Dean and Chapter, under the careful superintendence of Mr. Purday. (*See Arch. Inst. Journal,* 1859, p. 373.)

VII. From the Eden to the Solway Firth.

Westward of Carlisle the Wall is not easily traced. Having attained the high ground near what was the canal basin, it runs along the southern bank of the river as far as Grinsdale. The traces of it now are very slight. Hence, to Kirkandrews, it still adheres to the cliffs, though the river

Wall westward of the engine-sheds.

runs deviously in the flats to the north. The Vallum, instead of following closely the variations of the high ground, runs in a straight line past Mill-beck to Kirkandrews. The church-yard at Kirkandrews is a mass of stones; it has probably been the site of a mile-castle. In a garden in the village of Kirkandrews is preserved an altar which was found at Kirksteads, about a mile south of the Wall. What remains of the inscription may be translated—" Lucius Junius Victorinus and Caius Ælianus, Imperial Legates, (belonging) to the sixth legion, (styled) the victorious, the dutiful, and the faithful, (erected this altar) on account of achievements prosperously performed beyond the Wall." It is represented on the previous page. In crossing the beck, before approaching Beaumont, the fosse of the Wall is well developed. Here again the quantity of stones in the church-yard indicates an unusual amount of building.

Kirkandrews.

Beaumont.

The Wall, which had pursued a north-west direction to reach Beaumont, now resumes its westerly course, and may be traced all the way to Burgh-upon-Sands, and thence to Dikesfield, selecting with care every eminence it meets. The Vallum pursues a nearly direct course from Kirkandrews to Burgh-upon-Sands. A little to the west of Monk Hill, it crosses the turnpike road, and keeps on the north side of it nearly all the way to Burgh-upon-Sands.

Burgh-upon-Sands.

The station described.

Here we have another station of about three acres in extent. It is about five miles and a half from Stanwix. The outlines of the station are not well defined. It has, no doubt, extended a little to the north of the present turnpike road, and has had the Wall for its northern rampart. The church is within its eastern boundary; a road running north and south probably indicates its western wall. The Vallum has, as usual, come up to its southern rampart. In the church-yard frequent indications of Roman occupation are turned up.

The church at Burgh-upon-Sands, of the construction of which the wood-cut gives a general idea, is a good specimen The church.

of the fortified border churches. This church has some traces of Norman work, (as in the doorway on its north side), but the church was almost wholly rebuilt in the thirteenth century. The tower at the west end evidently has been a place of refuge. Its walls are seven feet thick. Instead of a large arch (as is usual) opening into the tower from the nave, a small door-way, guarded by a ponderous iron door, gives access to the vaulted chamber on the ground-floor of this

Its two towers.

fortress tower. "The ground-floor chamber being vaulted, would be secure against fire, and in the event of the door being forced and the lower story carried, the newel-staircase could still be strongly barricaded; thus, as it would only admit of one person ascending at a time, a stout resistance could be made, whilst the bells would be rung to give an alarm, and call to the rescue any succour that might be at hand." (*Arch. Inst. Journal*, 1859, p. 320.) There was formerly a tower at the east end of the church, which may have been the residence of the vicar. Being in a dilapidated state, in 1704 Bishop Nicholson recommended its removal, and the construction of a school-house instead; it is now used as a vestry.

Burgh Marsh.

To the north of the village is Burgh Marsh, on which Edward I. and his army were encamped, waiting for a favourable opportunity to cross the Solway, when death seized that monarch, on the 7th July, 1307. The monument here represented marks the spot where he succumbed.

Tower of Repentance. On the northern bank of the Solway is a beacon called the Tower of Repentance. It was erected by a conscience-stricken marauder, who, on a stormy passage from the English to the other side of the Firth, threw his prisoners overboard in preference to the cattle which he had stolen.

From Burgh-on-the-Sands to Bowness.

Watch-hill. From Burgh the Wall passes by West-end farm-house to Watch-hill; an accumulation of small stones renders it probable that a mile-castle stood here. It then makes straight for the edge of the marsh at Dykesfield. The Vallum is traceable at intervals throughout this distance. **A final adieu to the Vallum.** It is seen for the last time about fifty yards north of the public road, south of Watch-hill. Mr. McLauchlan could not ascertain the point where it joined the marsh. **Dykesfield.** At Dykesfield is a fragment of a small altar to the mother goddesses, found on

Altars. the spot, and at Longburgh is a small altar to Belatucader, also found in the neighbourhood.

Although the Wall, when last seen both at Dykesfield and Drumburgh, seems to be making straight for the opposite side of the marsh, there can be little doubt that it skirted its southern margin, going round by Boustead-hill and Easton. No traces of it remain.

Drumburgh station.

At Drumburgh is a station—the smallest on the line—containing an area of only three-quarters of an acre. It is four miles and a quarter from Burgh. South of the station is a well, said to be Roman, from which the water is now drawn by a pump. In the farm-yard at Drumburgh is a stone, with Norman tracery upon it, seemingly derived from some ecclesiastical structure. The castle here, of which there are considerable remains, is a fine specimen of the fortified manor-house of the olden time. Leland, writing of it

The Manor house.

in 1539, says:—"At Drumburygh, the Lord Dacre's father builded upon old ruines a prety pyle for defence of the country. The stones of the Pict Wall were pulled down to build it."

In cutting the canal (now the railway), in the vicinity of Glasson, a prostrate forest of considerable extent was met with. "Although the precise period when this forest fell is not ascertainable, there is positive proof that it must have been prior to the building of the Wall, because the foundations of the Wall passed obliquely over it, and lay three or four feet above the level of the trees." Much of the timber was sound; some of it was used in forming the jetty at Port Carlisle. Primeval forest.

The Wall, after leaving Burgh, bends to the north of Glasson, keeping to the south of the road, and having reached the shore, runs along it past Westfield and Kirkland to Port Carlisle. Occasionally traces of it are discernible. The mound called Fisher's Cross would be an admirable site for a mile-castle, and may have been one. Over the inn door at Port Carlisle is the fragment of an altar, having the letters MATRIBVS SVIS, a dedication, doubtless, to the *deæ matres*. The site of the Wall may be traced from this point nearly all the way to Bowness. Besides its foundation, the north fosse occasionally appears. The Wall here, when first seen by the writer, was several feet high. On the right hand, close by the shore, is another barrow-like object, called Knock's Cross. "As old as Knock's Cross" is a local proverb. "The water-course to a mill [now disused], leading straight to the entrance to Bowness, probably occupies the site of the fosse of the Wall." (*Mem.*, p. 87.) Glasson. Fisher's Cross. Knock's Cross.

The station of Bowness is well situated. It stands upon a bow-shaped promontory, round which the waters of the Solway bend, and are then lost in the Irish Channel. Its platform is slightly elevated above the general level of the sur- Station of Bowness.

rounding country. The station is not made out without difficulty. Its northern wall has stood upon the ridge overlooking the estuary. An ancient mound, still known to a few as the Rampire, or Rampart-head, is just outside its eastern rampart. Its western rampart is easily detected; and its south-west angle may, though with difficulty, be noticed. Although the form of the ground might lead to a different conclusion, the church is to the south of the station, and is not included in its area. The greatest length of the station is from east to west. It contains an area of five acres and a half. Its distance from Drumburgh is three miles and three-quarters nearly. Over a stable-door, about the middle of the town, is the small altar here engraved. It is a dedication to Jupiter for the welfare of the Emperors Gallus and Volusianus.

Rampart-head.

Our last altar.

At Wallsend we found that the eastern wall of the station was continued down the hill to a point below low water mark in the river Tyne; a similar arrangement prevailed here. Mr. McLauchlan says "Beyond Bowness we find no satisfactory account of the continuance of the Wall, though the old inhabitants point out at about 250 yards from the north-west angle of the station, a spot where a quantity of stone was dug out of the beach many years since, for building purposes, and the line of it was followed for some distance under the sand, without arriving at the end of it. The direction of these remains, as pointed out by the old people, would fall in with a continuation of

The Wall stretching into the sea.

the north front for about 100 yards, thence down a natural ridge, well suited to a line of defence, and on the south of the school-house, into the water."

At first sight Camden thought that the Solway was a sufficient defence, and that the Wall need not have been taken thus far; his words are (as rendered by Holland)—"I marvailed at first, why they built here so great fortifications, considering that for eight miles or thereabout, there lieth opposite a very great frith and arme of the sea; but now I understand that every ebbe the water is so low, that the Borderers and beast-stealers may easily wade over."

Why the Wall went so far.

Although a little to the east of the station, the Solway is easily fordable at low water, no one in the memory of the inhabitants of the place, has forded the estuary westward of the town. This circumstance would render Bowness a fit place at which to terminate the Wall of Hadrian.

The present repose of Bowness seems to contrast strangely with the bustle which must have reigned in it, when so large a station was fully occupied by Roman troops. The little town is the resort, during the summer season, of families for the purpose of sea-bathing.

Ancient and modern Bowness.

If the pilgrim who has followed the Wall from its eastern to its western extremity has enjoyed favourable weather, he will doubtless regret the termination of his labours. One consolation remains to him. The Wall was supported, both on its northern and southern margins, by stations of considerable importance, and to these he may now direct his attention.

CHAPTER IV.

SUPPORTING STATIONS.

IN order rightly to estimate the strength of the Roman Wall, we must take into account the stationary camps which existed both to the north and the south of it. Against these the wave of hostile aggression, in either direction, would, in the first instance, strike.

The estuary of the Tyne.

The estuary of the Tyne was strongly fortified. There is no doubt that there was a camp at Tynemouth, and another at the west end of North Shields, though no traces of them are now to be found. There were also two on the opposite side of the estuary—one on the Law, at the east end of South Shields, and another at Jarrow. Some traces of these, though feeble, remain. The remains of Bede's church and monastery render a visit to Jarrow very interesting.

Chester-le-Street.

Chester-le-Street is about seven miles to the south of Newcastle. Its name indicates its Roman origin. The church, church-yard, and deanery gardens stand within the station. Numerous Roman remains have been found here.

Bremenium.

An important series of stations stand upon the Roman road called Watling Street. BREMENIUM, the modern High Rochester, is the most northerly. It is about twenty-two miles north of the Wall. The ramparts, ditches, and gates of the station are easily discernible. Some fine pieces of masonry remain. Extensive excavations were made here in 1852 by his Grace the Duke of Northumberland, and, more recently, by the Society of Antiquaries of Newcastle. Important discoveries were made, which are detailed in the *Arch. Æl.*, N.S., vol. i., p. 69. Although the excavations are now filled in, there is much in the station and its vicinity to gratify the antiquary. The earthen camps at Chew Green, on the Scottish side of the boundary-line, are very curious, and the Watling Street between Chew Green and Bremenium is in a better state of preservation than in any other part. There is excellent accommodation at the inn at Horsley, which is within a mile of the station of Bremenium. A mail-gig plies daily between Horsley and Newcastle, passing Otterburn on its way. Elsdon is within an easy walk of Otterburn. The Rectory, a fortified tower of the fourteenth century, and the Moat Hill, an immense earth-work, probably of the British period, but afterwards occupied by the Romans, are worthy of examination.

Chew Green

Elsdon.

Habitancum.

Rob of Risingham.

Following the Watling Street about seven miles southward, we come to HABITANCUM, the modern Risingham. The station is well defined. To the south of it is the rock on which the figure of the famous Rob of Risingham was sculptured. The upper half of him has been blasted off; the lower portion of his figure remains, as shewn in the woodcut on the preceding page.

Risingham is about three miles from the Bellingham station of the Border Counties Railway. By this route also Horsley, Otterburn, and Elsdon may be reached; and the Wansbeck Valley Railway, now in course of formation, will afford a still easier access to them.

CORSTOPITUM, Corbridge, is the next station on the Watling Street. (See p. 82.)

Ebchester.

Ebchester is the next. It may easily be reached by the coaches plying between Newcastle and Shotley Bridge. All its ramparts may be traced. The parish-church, built of Roman stones, stands within it. The turnpike-road crosses the station, probably on the very line of the *via principalis.*

Lanchester.

Lanchester is next in order. It can be approached from Newcastle and Durham by railway. Its remains are very encouraging, though they were more so a few years ago.

Binchester.

Binchester is still further south, on the same line of road. It is near Bishop Auckland, to which there is a railway. Within the station is the most perfect hypocaust in the North of England.

Pierse Bridge.

Pierse Bridge is on the north bank of the river Tees. The station is well defined. To this place also there is access by railway.

We now turn to the stations on the Maiden Way.

Bewcastle is difficult of access. A pedestrian can best reach it by taking his course across the moors. The turnpike-road is somewhat circuitous. Or it may be approached from Brampton. The camp occupies a platform slightly elevated above the rivulet Kirkbeck. It departs from the usual form of Roman camps, being six-sided. A ruined castle (Bueth's Castle) and the famous obelisk give additional interest to the place. Bewcastle.

Whitley Castle is the modern name of another out-post, which is situated as far south of the Wall as Bewcastle is north of it. It is near Alston, to which there is a branch line from Haltwhistle, on the Newcastle and Carlisle Railway. The form of the station is peculiar, being that of a trapezoid. In addition to the ordinary walls, it is defended, on the western side, which is the most exposed, by seven earthen ramparts, and on the north by four. The Maiden Way passes by the east side of the station. In the farmhouse here, called the Castle Nook, is preserved an altar, which is carved on all four sides. The inscription has been obliterated, but it has no doubt been dedicated to Apollo. Whitley Castle.

We now approach the western extremity of the line. Nearly due north from Carlisle, and not far from the Scottish frontier, is the station of Netherby. It is about a mile and a half from Longtown. The outline of the station is nearly obliterated. A number of very important inscribed and sculptured stones, derived from this station, are preserved in the Hall, the ancestral seat of the Grahams of Netherby. Netherby.

Nearly due north from Bowness, and near Ecclefechan in Dumfriesshire, is the station of Middleby. Its ramparts Middleby.

and gateways are distinct. Some altars and other antiquities found in it are preserved at Hoddam Castle.

There are some important stations south of the Wall. About two miles south of Wigton, in Cumberland, is a large and well-defined station, called Old Carlisle. Many of the inscriptions found in it are preserved in the grounds of Miss Aglionby, of Wigton.

Old Carlisle.

Maryport

On the cliffs overhanging the modern town of Maryport, are the manifest remains of a large Roman station. Its position gives it a commanding view of the Solway Firth and Irish Channel. The camp is a large one, and the lines of its ramparts are very boldly developed. The sill of the eastern gateway is deeply worn by the action of chariot-wheels. In the neighbouring mansion of Nether Hall, the seat of J. Pocklington Senhouse, Esq., is preserved a large and very important collection of inscriptions and other antiquities found in the station here.

Moresby.

At Moresby, within a short distance of Whitehaven, are the well-defined outlines of another Roman camp. It was partially excavated by Lord Lonsdale in 1860, but little of importance was found. The ramparts, and the walls of some buildings of the interior, were found standing about a yard high. A military-way ran along the coast from this station, by Maryport, to the extremity of the Wall at Bowness.

One object of the camps on the Cumbrian coast, no doubt, was to prevent the settlement of "Scots," who at that time "poured out of Ireland."

At a very short notice the garrisons of an extensive frontier could be concentrated on any one point.

CHAPTER V.

THE BUILDER OF THE WALL.

THE questions have been much discussed, "When was the Wall built, and Who was its builder?" The pilgrim will find it an agreeable exercise, whilst pursuing his journey, to ponder upon these subjects. The following statements may aid him in his meditations:—

Horsley's opinion.

Horsley conceived that the stations were built by Agricola, and that the north agger of the Vallum was constructed by him as a military-way to communicate with them. He thinks that the ditch of the Vallum and the mounds on each side of it were constructed by Hadrian, as his defence against the Caledonians, and that he availed himself of the previously existing road and stations of Agricola. He is further of opinion that the Wall, with its castles, turrets, and military-way are to be ascribed to Severus. Mr. McLauchlan adopts Mr. Horsley's views.

The views of Gildas and Bede.

According to Gildas and Bede, the Wall was not built either by Hadrian or Severus, but was the work of the fifth century. The Rev. Charles Merivale, the able author of *The History of the Romans under the Empire*, is of this opinion. In an article in the *Quarterly Review* (January, 1860), in which indulgent allusion is made to the present writer's labours, he thus states the case:—

"Early in the fourth century the island was overrun by the barbarians of Caledonia, whom we now first hear of under the name of Picts and Scots, and their predatory hordes were encountered by Theodosius, the general of the Emperor Valens, in the neighbourhood of London, in the year 368. The invaders were routed and driven back beyond both the limitary ramparts, and Theodosius restored, as we are expressly informed by a reputable historian, the camps, castles, and prætenturæ, or chains of forts in the north, and reconstituted the province beyond the Solway under the designation of Valentia. As, however, no prudent general could hope to retain the permanent occupation of this exposed district, it might be judged expedient to take this opportunity of securing the lower and more important line of defences by the strongest fortifications. If, hitherto, the bulwarks of the lower isthmus had been confined to the camps and mounds of Hadrian and Severus, it was now, we may suppose, that the stations were fenced with masonry, and the Wall designed and at least partly executed, with broad openings at every mile for the temporary shelter of the exposed provincials beyond it. After the retirement of Theodosius, the frontiers were again assailed by the restless savages. Stilicho, about 400, issued orders from Gaul for putting the island in a state of defence against the Saxons, the Picts, and the Scots, and if we may rely on the evidence of the poet Claudian, his designs were carried fully into execution. We may at least admit that his engineers continued and extended the plan of Theodosius. Finally, after the withdrawal of the Roman garrison by Maximus, the Picts and Scots repeated their attacks, and the single legion which was sent from Rome in 414, and again a few years later, may have assisted or at least advised the natives in putting the finishing stroke to their defensive works, and thus the Wall, the remains of which we now see, may have occupied, from first to last, fifty years in building."

Hadrian the builder.

A third view has been taken of this question, which is, that all the works form one design, and are necessarily the work of one period and one mind. Those who hold this view generally regard Hadrian as the builder. Stukeley says—"In my judgment the true intent both of Hadrian's Vallum and Severus's Wall was in effect to make a camp extending across the kingdom; consequently was fortified both ways, north and south." "Both works were made at the same time, and by the same persons." The Rev. John

Hodgson, near the close of his great work upon the Wall, says—"In the progress of the preceding investigations, I have gradually and slowly come to the conviction, that the whole Barrier between the Tyne at Segedunum and the Solway at Bowness, and consisting of the Vallum and the Murus, with all the castella and towers of the latter, and many of the stations on their line, were planned and executed by Hadrian; and I have endeavoured to show that in this whole there is unity of design, and a fitness for the general purposes for which it was intended, which I think would not have been accomplished if part of the Vallum had been done by Agricola, the rest of it by Hadrian, and the Murus, with its castella, towers, and military way by Severus." It is impossible in the space now at command fully to state the arguments by which these views are maintained; the writer will be excused if he dwells chiefly upon that which he conceives to be the true one.

Mr. Hodgson's statement.

There are no good grounds for supposing that Agricola formed an extensive chain of forts from sea to sea. Tacitus, referring to his exploits in the North of England, tells us—"By these measures, many states which till that day had acted on the defensive, gave hostages, laid their hostility aside, and were environed with stations and castles (*præsidiis castellisque circumdatæ*) with so much calculation and care, that no part of Britain hitherto unnoticed could escape unmolested." (*Vit Agric.* cap. 20.) Agricola, no doubt, secured the chief passes in the isthmus; but it is highly improbable that, at a time when he was flushed with success, and was contemplating the subjugation of Scotland, he would construct an elaborate fortification, consisting of

Agricola's chain of forts doubtful.

at least seventeen stations, connected together throughout the entire distance between the Tyne and the Solway Firth by a military-way.

The northern mound not paved.

The north agger of the Vallum, which is said to be Agricola's military-way, bears no marks of having been paved, and differs in no respect from the southernmost agger, which is confessedly nothing more than a rampart of earth.

The works do not cross each other.

It is worthy of observation, that the mound ascribed to Agricola, A.D. 79, the mounds and ditch ascribed to Hadrian, A.D. 120, and the Wall ascribed to Severus, A.D. 208, never cut in upon one another. If the northernmost agger were constructed as a road, and the southernmost agger were constructed forty years afterwards, for a very different purpose—as a base of operation against a foe, it is remarkable that they should run in lines perfectly parallel. Mr. McLauchlan remarks—"There are instances along the line where the Wall appears to have turned in its course for no other reason than to avoid running in upon the Vallum, on the supposition that the latter had been made first, as may be seen about 400 yards east of Heddon-on-the-Wall. . . Again at Newtown, about a mile west of Petriana." (*Mem.* p. 90.) Still, it is true that the works of the Wall and Vallum never cross each other. Had they been constructed by different engineers, and at different periods, especially if the later works, had been caused by the decay or inefficiency of the preceding ones, they assuredly would. Again, if in a few instances the Wall yields to the Vallum the point of advantage, this is the exception, and not the rule. For miles together the Vallum yields to the Wall the ground that is most suitable for operating against a northern foe. For miles together the Vallum is commanded by the Wall. Horsley fully admits this; he says, "It must be owned, that the southern prospect of Hadrian's work and the defence on that side is generally better than on the north; whereas the northern prospect and defence have been principally or only taken care of in the Wall of Severus." (p. 125.) Hadrian's engineers must have been great blunderers, and offended against the primary rule of castrametation, as laid down by Vegetius, "that care should be taken to have no neighbouring hill higher than the fortification, which, being seized by the enemy, might be of ill-consequence," or they had something else to depend upon besides the Vallum for beating off a northern enemy. The Vallum commanded by the Wall, on the north.

Again, on the supposition that Agricola built the stations, and reared the northern mound of the Vallum as a road to communicate with his chain of forts, how is it that Hadrian, when he found it necessary to add to the previously existing measures of defence against the Caledonians, did not draw his lines on the northern or exposed side of his camps and military-way? Men in presence of an enemy usually carry their shields in front of them, not behind their backs.

The reader will naturally ask, What say the ancient writers upon the question at issue? If their statements are not entirely satisfactory, they are at all events not inimical to the view here taken that Hadrian built the Wall. Two historians of note flourished during the reign of Severus—Dion Cassius and Herodian—and they both treat of British affairs. Dion Cassius twice mentions the Wall. Speaking of the state of things in the time of Commodus, he says, The ancient writers upon the question. Dion Cassius.

"Some of the nations within that island, having passed over the Wall which divided them from the Roman stations, . . . committed much devastation, &c." (*Monumenta Historica*, p. lix.) The other passage relates to the reign of Severus; "Among the Britons, the two greatest tribes are the Caledonians and the Meatæ. . . . The Meatæ dwell close to the Wall, which divides the island into two parts; the Caledonians beyond them." (*Mon. Hist.* p. lx.)

Herodian Herodian flourished about the year 238. The only reference which he makes to the Wall, is the following—"His (Severus's) army having passed beyond the rivers and fortresses which defended the Roman territory, there were frequent attacks and skirmishes, and retreats on the side of the barbarians."

These are the only passages that we have in the writings of any contemporary author; they are consistent with the idea that Hadrian built the Wall, but scarcely so with the supposition that Severus did so.

Spartian is the next writer who mentions the subject. He is not an author of much credit, and as he did not flourish till the close of the third century, his testimony is

Spartian. of the less value. Speaking of Hadrian, he says—"He sought Britain, where he corrected many things, and first drew a Wall (*murum duxit*) for eighty miles to separate the barbarians and the Romans." (*Mon. Hist.* p. lxv.) Writing of Severus, he says—"He secured Britain, which is the chief glory of his reign, having drawn a wall across the island (*muro per transversam insulam ducto*); whence he also received the name of Britannicus." (*Mon. Hist.* p. lxv.) Once more he mentions the Wall in connection with Severus—"After the Emperor had passed the Wall or Vallum (*post murum aut vallum missum*), and was returning to the nearest station," &c. (*Mon. Hist.* p. lxv.)

Julius Capitolinus.

Julius Capitolinus, who flourished at the close of the third century, in recording the erection of the Antonine Wall in Scotland, says—"Antoninus carried on many wars by his legates; for he conquered even the Britons by his legate, Lollius Urbicus; having, after driving back the barbarians, constructed another wall composed of turf, (*alio muro cespiticio ducto.*) (*Mon. Hist.*, p. lxv.)

These are the chief passages bearing upon the subject, and all, with one exception, that our space will admit of.

Testimony of inscriptions.

The argument on which the supporters of the claims of Hadrian chiefly rely, is the testimony of the inscriptions found upon the Wall. On the Wall itself, or in the stations immediately connected with it, not a single inscription to Severus has been found, whereas several have been met with mentioning the name of Hadrian or his contemporaries. At Procolitia, Vindolana, Æsica, and Petriana—all of them *stationes per lineam Valli*—indubitable references to Hadrian or his era have been found. In several of the supporting stations also inscriptions have been erected to his honour. Omitting, however, all reference to these, the following fact seems decisive. In four of the mile-castles between the stations of Borcovicus and Æsica, slabs or portions of slabs have been found recording the names of Hadrian and of his propraetor, Aulus Platorius Nepos. The mile-castles are confessedly an essential part of the Wall, and as in this part of the line the Wall is further removed from the Vallum than usual, and stands upon a higher elevation, it is not likely that these inscribed stones would be brought from the Vallum to it.

Inscriptions to Severus, in the supporting stations.

At Hexham, Risingham, and Old Carlisle, stations not immediately connected with the Wall, inscriptions to Severus have been met with. At Coome-crag and on the Gelt-rock are inscriptions belonging to the period when he was in Britain. Contemplating as he did the complete subjugation of Scotland, it is not probable that, before he went on his great enterprise, he would engage in so vast a work as the erection of the stone Wall, with its military-way and castles and turrets; and when he returned dispirited and virtually beaten, having lost fifty thousand men in the attempt, he would have neither time nor energy left for it. That in the prospect of his campaign he should take care that Hadrian's Wall, and the stations on his line of march, were put into an efficient state of repair, is quite natural; and that when he returned, after his three years' campaign, to York, to die, he should make every effort to render the Lower Isthmus secure, is equally probable. These operations are quite sufficient to account for some activity being exhibited in the quarries near the Wall in the time of Severus.

The opinion that the Wall was constructed in the fifth century, in consequence of orders sent to Britain by Stilicho, the prime minister of Honorius, is chiefly founded upon the following passage from Claudian:—

> "Me quoque vicinis pereuntem gentibus, inquit,
> Munivit Stilicho, totam cum Scotus Iernen
> Movit, et infesto spumavit remige Tethys
> Illius effectum curis, ne tela timerem
> Scotica, ne Pictos tremerem, neu litore tuto
> Prospicerem dubiis venturum Saxona ventis."

Though Claudian is a writer "who has indulged the most ample privilege of a poet and a courtier, some criticism is necessary to translate the language of fiction or exaggeration into the truth and simplicity of historic prose," yet Mr. Merivale thinks "we can hardly consent to regard the vigorous lines (now quoted) as mere rhetoric." With every wish to yield to Claudian the utmost credit that is due to him, the following considerations will press themselves upon the mind:—

Objections to the statements of Claudian.

1. Is it credible that so great a work as the Wall should be constructed when the Roman empire was in the very throes of dissolution—when the enemies, by which it was overthrown, were with difficulty kept out of Rome itself?

2. Is it likely that *orders* issued by Stilicho from the continent, supported as they were by the presence of but a single legion, would be sufficient to inspire the trembling natives of the island with energy enough to undertake this arduous work? This question will be perceived to have the more force when we remember that on former occasions the personal presence of the emperors themselves, or the active exertions of their most renowned generals, supported by three legions and numerous bodies of auxiliary troops, were considered necessary to drive back aggression and restore confidence to the friends of Rome.

3. It seems unaccountable that, under the pressing exigencies of the times, Rome should be able to spare a legion even for a short season; and knowing as we do the difficulties which attended the transport of a legion when the appliances of the empire were in a state of the highest efficiency, we are at a loss to understand how a legion could

once and again be sent from the heart of the empire to its extremity, and brought back again with the facility which the accounts of Claudian and Gildas seem to imply.

4. The masonry of the Wall is for the most part rough, but the whole structure has been so strong, that in many instances it has been necessary to have recourse to gunpowder, in order to effect its demolition. The masonry of some parts of the Barrier, however, as the bridge over the North Tyne, the north gateway of Borcovicus, and the gateways of the stations and mile-castles generally, will bear comparison with the best workmanship of the present day. Could such works have been erected in the gloomy times of Honorius?

5. The circumstance, that we meet with proofs along the whole line that the stations and castles have at different times been overthrown and re-edified, is best explained by the theory of the early construction of the Wall.

6. One other consideration is inimical to the view that Stilicho was the builder of the Wall. Upon the Wall itself, as well as in the stations, we meet with continually recurring records of the second, the sixth, and the twentieth legions; if the Wall was built by the panic-stricken Britons, under the guidance of one legion, what legion was it, and how is it that we have numerous memorials, not of one, but three?

Conclusion. This chapter cannot be further prolonged. Whatever decision the reader may come to, he will not be unwilling to look upon the portrait of Hadrian copied from one of his coins, which is subjoined. "Hadrian died," Mr. Merivale tells us, "on the tenth day of July, A.D. 138." Among his last words, delivered perhaps in a brief interval of ease, was a playful address to his departing spirit, which Mr. Merivale thus happily renders—

> " Soul of mine, pretty one, flitting one,
> Guest and partner of my clay,
> Whither wilt thou hie away,—
> Pallid one, rigid one, naked one—
> Never to play again, never to play?"

Character of Hadrian.

" On the whole," says this erudite author, " I am disposed to regard the reign of Hadrian as the best of the imperial series, marked by endeavours at reform and improvement in every department of administration in all quarters of the Empire." Speaking of his person and countenance, he says— " He reminds us more than any Roman before him of what we proudly style the thorough English gentleman."

CHAPTER VI.

THE ANTIQUITIES FOUND ON THE WALL.

Many specimens have been given in the course of the preceding pages of the most important class of antiquities found upon the Wall—altars, dedicatory slabs, and centurial stones. Gold coins are extremely rare; many silver pieces have been found; the copper and brass coins that have been picked up are for the most part very highly corroded. Finger rings of gold, silver, bronze, iron, and jet are occasionally dug up. There is set in many of those rings an artificial stone, on which some design is roughly but effectively cut. Fibulæ or brooches, generally of bronze, for the fastening of the woollen garments of the men, as well as women, are also found. The wood-cut shows some specimens from the collection at Walton House.

Altars and inscriptions.

Fibulæ.

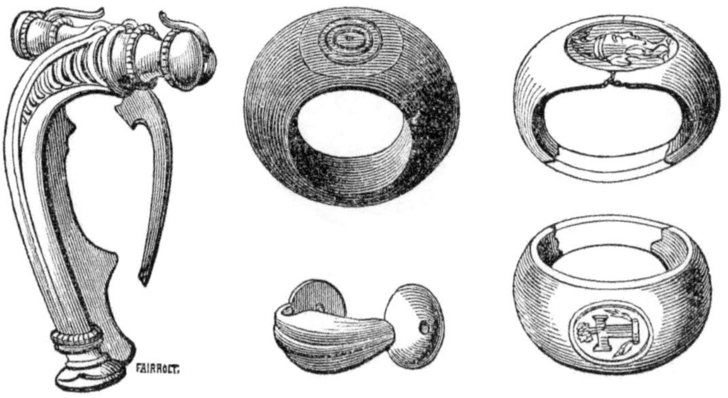

If the object shown in this wood-cut, be as it appears a vinegaret, it shows that the elegancies of life were not, even in those days of fierce conflict, banished from the region of the Wall. If modern locksmiths had but studied Roman antiquities, they would have found a royal road to some of their modern inventions. Here is a key of elaborate form intended to be worn as a ring upon the finger; it is from the museum at Chesters. Other minor articles.

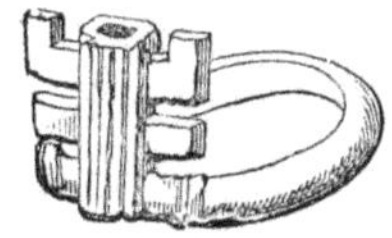

Pottery, usually forms an abundant class of Roman relics in every camp that has been long occupied. The Samian ware is very beautiful, and very characteristic. It is sometimes embossed, as in the specimen here given, but more Pottery.

frequently plain. This species of "ware" has been imported from the continent. Other kinds are common, and were probably of native manufacture. Amongst them may be noticed the *mortarium*, a strong shallow dish with a spout (of which there is a specimen in the centre of the cut), which was used for gently bruising their food in, and

was also occasionally thrust amongst the embers as a stew-pan. Fragments of wine amphoræ are not uncommon. Glass vessels are occasionally met with, but they are rare.

Conclusion. The writer would now withdraw—hoping that the pilgrim, for whose benefit he has, not without some toil and much anxiety penned these pages, may be strong of limb and joyous of heart,—that the heavens may be propitious, and that every step of his journey may yield him knowledge, and help him on in that great pilgrimage which we have come into this world to accomplish!

"I do love these ancient ruins:
We never tread upon them, but we set
Our feet upon some reverend history.
. . . . But all things have their

END."

INDEX.

Newcastle-upon-Tyne: Printed by J. G. Forster, 81, Clayton Street.

For EU product safety concerns, contact us at Calle de José Abascal, 56–1°,
28003 Madrid, Spain or eugpsr@cambridge.org.

www.ingramcontent.com/pod-product-compliance
Ingram Content Group UK Ltd.
Pitfield, Milton Keynes, MK11 3LW, UK
UKHW010342140625
459647UK00010B/769

* 9 7 8 1 1 0 8 0 8 0 6 6 8 *